CLASSIC
SPANISH
COOKING
WITH
CHEF EF

CLASSIC
SPANISH
COOKING
WITH
CHEF EF

by
Efraín Martínez

Illustrations by
Eric S. Angeloch

LOWELL HOUSE
LOS ANGELES

CONTEMPORARY BOOKS
CHICAGO

Library of Congress Cataloging-in-Publication Data

Martinez, Efrain.
    Classic Spanish cooking with Chef Ef / by Efrain Martinez.
       p.   cm.
    Includes index.
    ISBN 1-56565-084-0
    1. Cookery, Spanish.   I. Title.
TX723.5.S7M358   1993
641.5946—dc20   93-20469
                                   CIP

Requests for such permissions should be addressed to:
Lowell House
2029 Century Park East, Suite 3290
Los Angeles, CA 90067

PUBLISHER: Jack Artenstein

VICE-PRESIDENT/EDITOR-IN-CHIEF: Janice Gallagher

DIRECTOR OF PUBLISHING SERVICES: Mary D. Aarons

TEXT DESIGN: Stanley S. Drate/Folio Graphics Co. Inc.

Manufactured in the United States of America

10   9   8   7   6   5   4   3   2   1

Contents

ARAGÓN

CATALONIA

THE BALEARIC ISLANDS

THE CANARY ISLANDS

MENU SUGGESTIONS 237

SPANISH WINES, SHERRIES, AND LIQUEURS 243

Dedication

I want to dedicate this book in memory of my dear grandmother, Doña Felicita Pérez de García, for her inspiration in Spanish cooking.

Acknowledgments

JOANNE

My wife, for supporting me through my ups and downs. I love you.

JOSEFINA GARCÍA

My mother, who never asked me to get a real job.

GIANCARLO, LISA, and MICHAEL

My son and stepchildren, for being samplers of my cuisine.

LUZ DELIA, NOEMA, DELIA, and AMERICA

My aunts, for their traditional recipes.

DON JOSE del CARMEN GARCÍA

My grandfather, for his wise words.

LUIS MARTÍNEZ

My father, for being part of me.

TO ALL MY CLOSEST FRIENDS FOR THEIR LOVE AND SUPPORT

Rosane and Santiago, Carole and Vinny, Stacy and Lenny, Vicky and George. *Gracias*.

STEPHEN HONEYBILL and TOM MERKLINGER

The producer and director of WMHT-TV 17, Schenectady, New York, for their support.

JAMES MOORE

Director of production of WNYT-TV 13, Albany, New York, for planting the seed.

ALL THE STAFF AT WMHT-TV 17

For helping to consume all that food we cooked during the taping of "Classic Spanish Cooking with Chef Ef."

GLORIA FILERINO

My assistant chef, for helping put together all those wonderful dishes.

PETER and CHERYL COLLETTI

From Magefesa Cookware for supplying me with their excellent pressure cooker.

PEDRO PEREA

From Magefesa for his hints in Spanish cooking.

HARRY KOETSENRUYTER

From Magefesa for not asking me to pronounce his last name. Thank you, Harry.

ALL THE PEOPLE FROM MAGEFESA

For their underwriting support to the series "Classic Spanish Cooking with Chef Ef." Thank you.

JOSE IGNACIO DOMECQ (DOMECQ IMPORTERS)

Thank you for that excellent Spanish wine you gave us and for supporting "Classic Spanish Cooking with Chef Ef." *Gracias.*

TO ALL THESE RESTAURANTS FOR THEIR CONTRIBUTIONS:

Cafe Ba-Ba-Reeba
Chicago, IL, USA

Centro Vasco Restaurant
New York, NY, USA

El Meson Madrid
Palisades Park, NJ, USA

Emiliòs Tapas Bar
Chicago, IL, USA

La Paella Restaurant
Chicago, IL, USA

Ramiro's Restaurant
Coral Gables, FL, USA

Botafumeiro Galician Cooking
Barcelona, Spain

Hosteria Pintor Zuloaga
Segovia, Spain

La Balsa Restaurant
Barcelona, Spain

Las Delicias Restaurant
Asturias, Spain

Parador Duques de Cardona
Barcelona, Spain

Parador Luís Vives
Valencia, Spain

Parador Monte Perdido
Aragón, Spain

Parador Molino Viejo
Asturias, Spain

Parador Nacional Principe de Viana
Navarra, Spain

Parador Nacional Vía de la Plata
Extremadura, Spain

Restaurante de Siete Portes
Barcelona, Spain

Ancora Restaurant
Palma de Mallorca, Balearics

El Gállo Restaurant
Palma de Mallorca, Balearics

Valparaiso Restaurant
Palma de Mallorca, Balearics

El Acuario Restaurant
Las Palmas, Gran Canaria

Parador de Argomaniz
Basque Country

Special Thanks

I want to thank Barry Ballister for his writing talent and assistance. When I created the idea for "Chef Ef" I asked Barry to assist me in developing the TV series and the book. His experience and his understanding of my thoughts and dreams, along with the ability to re-create them in words, helped produce the television shows and the book. We have been able to combine our backgrounds, experiences, and talents to bring you a deep insight into the history, romance, and culinary art of one of the world's great cultures. *Gracias, amigo.*

Barry Ballister is the author of *Barry Ballister's Fruit and Vegetable Stand.*

My Classic Spanish Upbringing

It seems as if I've been in the kitchen my whole life—and loving it. I was born in New York City to Josefina García Perez and Luís Martínez Negrón, descendants of Spanish families from the regions of San Andrés in Andalucia and Tenerife in the Canary Islands.

I was very young when my family moved back to San Andrés in the south of Spain and I fell under the wonderful spell of my grandmother, Doña Felicita Pérez de García. My earliest memories are of her kitchen filled with the aroma of Spanish olive oil and garlic. To me, it was her perfume. During the time I lived with my grandmother, every meal was another Spanish feast. She created fish, meat, and vegetable dishes that reflected the bounty, variety, and history of Spanish cooking. Her recipes came from all over Spain and carried the influences of Roman, Arab, and African conquerors. Our close relationship awakened me to the virtues of classic Spanish food.

From San Andrés my family moved to San Juan de Puerto Rico. After 13 years of Caribbean island life, I returned to the United States, where I opened a catering business in Monticello, New York, providing authentic Spanish food to workers in the area, many of whom were of Spanish origin. The culinary seed sprouted and I developed a strong desire to open a restaurant that reflected my background in classic Spanish cooking. I felt I had to make everyone aware of the beauty and variety of Spanish food. I wanted people to realize the difference between the New World foods of Mexico and South America and the cuisine of Spain that began as far back as the Roman conquest.

My catering experience, together with all those years in my grandmother's kitchen and her wonderful recipes, gave me the tools and motivation to create La Posada, a Spanish restaurant in Saugerties, New York. At La Posada, Efraín Martínez became Chef Ef. I was renamed by my wife and children, who kept hearing people struggle with my given name. The public loved it, I loved it, and it stuck.

The menu at La Posada incorporated recipes from my grandmother and her grandmother, my aunts and their aunts, and other members of my family and friends who had been creating classic Spanish meals for generations. I translated menus from *Libre de Coch*, the first cookbook published in Spain in 1477 and written by Ruperto de Nola, chef to the king of Catalonia. The menu presented Spanish food in its enormous variety, colorful presentation, and depth of flavor. I cannot tell you how many of my customers came in looking for tacos and chimichangas and left as converts to the culinary experience of Setas Salteadas, Langosta y Pollo Catalan, and Tocino del Ciélo (all to be found in this book).

At La Posada I developed two special sauces. One was a parsley-based salsa verde and the other a tomato-based saffron red sauce. They became very popular and customers requested sauces to take home. I began packaging the salsa verde and the saffron sauce under the label La Mancha. The name reflected the image of the historic man of La Mancha, Don Quixote. I related to the Spanish hero, because like him, I had the desire to fulfill a dream, a dream to make everyone aware of the art and history of Spanish cooking. Everything I did with food became a testimony to one of the great cuisines of the world.

The salsas became a business, and I created a short video "infomercial" called "Spanish Cooking with Chef Ef" to help promote their sale. During the video production the director of WNYT Television in Albany, New York, James Moore, suggested that I develop a Spanish cooking television show for the American audience. With the assistance of Barry Ballister I created "Classic Spanish Cooking with Chef Ef," which was produced by the Public Broadcast Service for its network. As part of the creative effort I wrote this book, which reflects the theme and personality of the TV show, including many of the ancestral and historic recipes from my collection.

It is my dream and desire for you to enjoy this book and what it offers you in history, wine selection, and classic Spanish cuisine. In addition, I wish you all *salud, amor, dinero, y tiempo para disfrutarlo*, which means "health, love, money, and the time to enjoy it."

Introducing the Cuisine of Spain

Spanish cooking is historic. The combination of tremendous natural food resources and many cultural influences from Greece, Rome, Africa, and Europe has created a highly imaginative, colorful cuisine on the highest level of excellence. From the famous Spanish appetizers, *tapas*, to the extensive selection of pastries and desserts, no cuisine does so many things so well. Every region of Spain has its own special style of culinary art. The climate, geography, and cultural influences of each region have contributed to unique regional recipes, while classic, traditional customs have maintained other recipes that are the same throughout the entire country.

There are over 1,500 recipes for paella. Variations depend on whether the area produces more meat or more fish, poultry or game, root vegetables or leafy greens or both. The rice and saffron are constant, of course, but the finished paella is restricted only by the chef's preferences and the available ingredients. Chorizo, the famous Spanish sausage, has as many different varieties as there are people making it. Yet dishes like Pollo Chilindron, Langosta al Ajo Arriero, and Gazpacho Andalúz use basically the same recipes that have been around for centuries.

The Spanish kitchen uses everything from tiny, tender potatoes to whole lambs and suckling pigs. Fruits, vegetables, legumes, fish and shellfish, wild game and meats of all kinds are part of the Spanish cuisine. Many recipes are complicated and use 20 to 30 ingredients. Today's home chef has neither the time nor general inclination to devote to the preparation of some of these elaborate classic Spanish dishes. This book is created to preserve the flavor and character of traditional Spanish cooking with up-to-date techniques that simplify the process without sacrificing the unique character and flavors produced by classic Spanish recipes.

The food processor and blender are not only modern, convenient substitutes for the mortar and pestle, the hand grinder and grater, and endless chopping by hand—they are improvements that add to the textures, tastes, and color of Spanish food. Modern ovens, easy-to-control stove tops, electric grinders, and high-quality cookware only add to the excellence of classic Spanish recipes.

This book is a collection of dishes from Spain that were created long before Mexican, Cuban, and South American cooking projected an image of Spanish food as a collection of beans, rice, chili, and flaming hot sauces. As an historic collection of classic Spanish recipes, re-created for today's tastes, it presents an opportunity for you to sample some of the best cuisines from a country where food is a passion and a pleasure.

The culinary journey through Spain begins in the warm southeast from Levante and Andalucía, through the central regions, then northwest and east to Catalonia with a final trip into the Mediterranean and Spain's islands.

How to Reduce Fat, Salt, and Cholesterol and Still Cook Classic Spanish

One day a friend who was visiting my house asked me if she could make a paella Valenciana with no salt and lowered fat and still make a delicious, authentic meal. I suggested that she use fresh cilantro, increase the garlic and onions, and eliminate the salt entirely. She could reduce the fat by removing the skin from the chicken and cut down the oil significantly by using a nonstick pan. A week later she called me and told me excitedly how delicious her low-fat, no-salt paella Valenciana was. Likewise, with a few easy substitutions you can help your health and still create classic Spanish dishes.

1. Substitute olive oil for butter.
2. Reduce the amount of olive oil or butter.
3. Use nonstick utensils.
4. Substitute 1% milk or skim milk for milk or cream.
   Note: If you choose lower-fat substitutes for milk or cream, your sauces will not have the desired thickness. To compensate for this, I suggest you mix a thickener like arrowroot, cornstarch, or quick mixing flour into the milk or cream substitute. Mix and blend well before adding to the recipe. I do not, however, recommend substitutions for milk or cream in dessert recipes.
5. Salt to taste or eliminate the salt and increase the herbs and spices.
6. Don't use margarine.
7. Skim beef and chicken broth or substitute a mixture of cumin and water. Allow mixture to sit for about 10 minutes.
8. Use egg substitute in place of whole eggs.
9. Don't let your olive oil smoke.
10. Broil, don't fry.

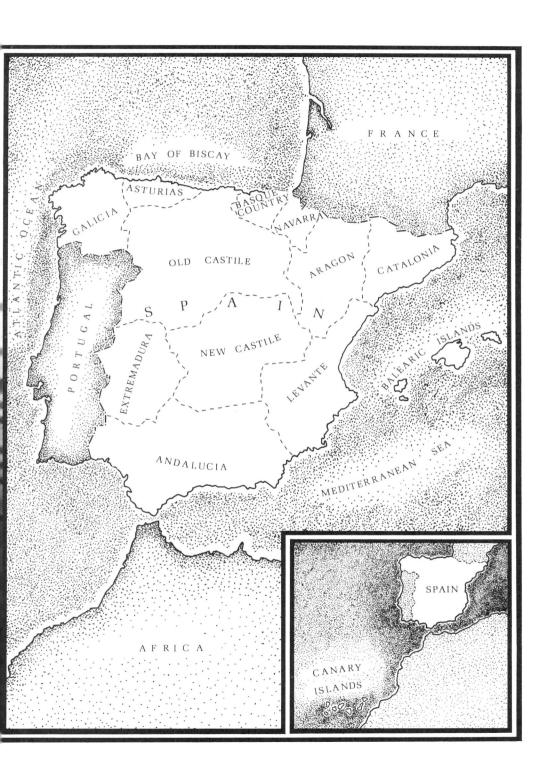

Valencian Rice Fields

LEVANTE

Levante is the land of the sunrise. It stretches northward along Spain's eastern coast and inland to the mountains. Between the sea and mountains rises a high plateau dense with orange and lemon groves, sugar cane, rice fields, and palms. And everywhere there are vegetable gardens. Tiny ones are tucked between the white stucco houses of the fishing villages. Cities are ringed with farms that produce abundant yields from the region's two-crop seasons. In the broad flatlands, plastic-sheeted commercial farms force incredible specimens of beautiful vegetables. During the different harvests the roads are choked with trucks heavy with beans, peas, potatoes, tomatoes, and peppers in all colors on their way to market.

In the area of Murcia the farms give way to orchards. Oranges are king with two crops of the sweet Valencia orange providing a year-round supply. The sweet blossoms fill the air with a heady perfume that leaves the visitor locked into a sensual memory. There are lemons and limes; abundant green and black figs; exotic fruit trees flourish with heavy clusters of dates, pomegranates, passionfruit, loquats, and tiny tangerine-like oranges called clementines, a seedless mandarin orange shipped all over the world.

The seacoast is home to some of the world's richest fishing grounds. The fish markets of the Levante port cities are dazzling displays of giant prawns, red mullet, blue crabs, lobsters, huge sea bass, giant squid, and tiny sardines. Every variety and size is represented, and they all find their way into the imagination and the recipes of this food-oriented culture.

But above all, more than the fruit and cornucopia of vegetables, greater than the abundance of the Mediterranean, Levantian cuisine is represented by rice. Rice was planted in the eighth century by the Moors, who utilized the irrigation and aqueduct systems of the

1

Romans. It is the daily food of the Levantian people. It was rice that inspired the creation of paella, the national dish of Spain and recognized throughout the world as a standard of creative, classic cuisine. Interestingly enough, the word *paella* has nothing to do with the assortment of ingredients, but refers to the two-handled shallow pan of original Roman design that was called, in Latin, *patella*.

The original paella contained only eels, snails, shellfish, and green peas in addition to rice and saffron. But today every form of meat, fish, shellfish, and vegetable is a candidate for paella. The basic ingredient, however, is the rice: tender, fluffy, and individual grains. It is the rice that determines the great paellas. In Levante rice also stands on its own, often served by itself cooked in orange juice, cider, chicken stock, tomato juice, or fish stock.

The enormous agricultural wealth of the region, combined with the abundant seafood and natural game of duck, hare, and deer, along with traditional meats, poultry, and sausage, have inspired recipes full of imagination, variety, and pleasure.

Once again the history of Spain with all its invaders and re-conquerors is reflected in the cuisine of each region. From the early Roman waterworks through the cultural and philosophical expansion of the Arab rulers, to the liberation of Valencia by El Cid and the development of its God-given resources, Levante faces the sunrise every day with gusto and vitality and sets its tables with the finest food found anywhere.

THE WINES OF LEVANTE

The wines of Levante are produced in five separate regions in huge amounts, most of it for everyday drinking.

The region of Valencia extends from the semitropical climate of the coastal areas inland to the gentler, cooler hill country. Fresh, fruity whites with a greenish cast are made from the Merseguera grape; a heavier, fuller white wine is made from a mix of the Merseguera and Ximénez grapes. Farther south the area produces excellent sweet red Muscatel and a sugary, deep-red wine a la Chianti.

On the road from Valencia to Madrid lie two very old towns:

Utiel and Requena. The area of these villages produces an intense, thick, almost black wine with an interesting combination of sweetness and acidity. It is called *vino a doble pasta*. It is the result of the crushed black grapes fermenting after the initial pressing is drawn off. This high-alcohol wine is used for blending with thinner wines from northern regions. The wine that was drained from the initial pressing is allowed to ferment and produces a pale rosé that is exceptionally light, fruity, and delicate.

Inland from the city of Alicante are the vineyards of Villena and Monóvar. Wines are blended here by mixing small amounts of the sweet, high-sugar wines with higher amounts of the more robust varieties. Though some white wines are produced, the typical wines of Alicante are dark red in color and high in alcohol content. Yecla and Fumilla remain in the traditional past of winemaking. These two regions produce strong, full-bodied red wines from the Monastrel grape grown on the original ungrafted Spanish vine stock. The deep, dark wines, sold mostly in the domestic market, cling to the glasses they are served in. New technology and blending techniques will soon transform these regions' strong, high-alcohol wines into a lighter, more universally appreciated product.

Appetizers / Tapas

CLAMS IN CHILI SAUCE
ALMEJAS CALIENTES

This excellent tapa is for those who love spicy food. Prepared with crushed red pepper, olive oil, and fresh garlic, it is muy caliente.

SERVES 4

3	tablespoons olive oil
3	cloves garlic, mashed
½	cup chopped onion
2	tablespoons chopped fresh cilantro
½	teaspoon crushed red pepper
½	cup (4 oz.) dry white wine
1¼	cups canned crushed tomatoes
½	tablespoon flour
	Salt to taste
	Freshly ground pepper
24	small clams, well scrubbed
2	tablespoons chopped parsley for garnish

In a large skillet, heat the olive oil and sauté the garlic, onion, cilantro, and the crushed red pepper until the onion is soft. Add the wine, tomatoes, and flour and mix well until sauce begins to thicken. Add salt and pepper to taste and mix well. Add the clams to the sauce, cover, and cook over medium-high heat for about 5 minutes or until clams open. Remove the clams to a serving bowl. Mix the sauce well and pour over the clams. Sprinkle with the chopped parsley and serve hot.

MUSHROOMS WITH GARLIC AND SAUSAGE
SETAS SALTEADAS

This is one of the most popular tapas in the region of Levante. It is easy to prepare, and with a touch of brandy this dish is "madre mia, muy delicioso."

SERVES 4

2   tablespoons olive oil
3   cloves garlic, mashed
¼   cup chopped chorizo
3   tablespoons chopped flat parsley
2   tablespoons chopped onion
½   pound small mushrooms, whole, stems removed
¼   cup (2 oz.) brandy
2   tablespoons chopped parsley for garnish

In a large skillet, heat the oil and sauté the garlic, chorizo, flat parsley, onion, and mushrooms for about 5 minutes or until onion is soft. Add the brandy and flambé until flames subside (be very careful).

Remove the mixture to a serving platter and garnish with the remaining chopped parsley.

ANCHOVY SPREAD
CANAPE DE ANCHOA

This tapa comes from the Luís Vives Villa in Valencia, one of the government-designated historic villas now utilized as inns, bed-and-breakfast stopovers, or inexpensive lodgings called paradors. Once you try this dish you will long for a visit to the famous villa where the recipe was created.

SERVES 4

2   whole roasted pimentos, drained and chopped
4   ounces flat fillet anchovies, drained
½   cup chopped onion
1   clove garlic, peeled
2   tablespoons chopped fresh cilantro
1   teaspoon red wine vinegar
     Freshly ground pepper
2   tablespoons virgin olive oil
     Round salted crackers

In a food processor or blender, add all the ingredients except the crackers and blend well until a fine paste has formed. Transfer mixture to a serving bowl and refrigerate. Spread the mixture over the crackers and serve.

Vegetables / Legumbres

SAUTÉED ARTICHOKES
ALCACHOFAS SALTEADAS

The lush region of Levante provides some of the most exciting vegetables in all of Spain. In this classic artichoke recipe, the addition of chorizo and serrano ham creates a sizzling, hearty dish that will enhance the rest of the meal.

SERVES 4

- ¼   cup olive oil
- ¼   cup chopped serrano or prosciutto ham
- ¼   cup chopped chorizo
- ½   cup (4 oz.) dry white wine
- 1   pound fresh artichoke hearts, coarsely chopped
  Salt to taste
  Freshly ground pepper
- 3   tablespoons chopped parsley for garnish

In a large skillet, heat the olive oil and sauté the ham and chorizo until they begin to sizzle. Add the wine, artichoke, salt, and pepper and cook for about 3 minutes, mixing well.

Cover and cook over low heat for about 10 minutes until the artichokes are just tender. Remove to a serving platter and garnish with chopped parsley.

This dish can be served as a light meal or lunch.

LIMA BEANS AND CHORIZO
HABAS CON CHORIZOS

Lima beans are one of the healthiest vegetables grown anywhere. I suggest tiny limas for their sweetness. The contrast with the tangy chorizo makes this an interesting and compelling dish in any meal.

SERVES 4

8 cups water
1 pound fresh shelled lima beans
1 tablespoon olive oil
¼ cup chopped chorizo
1 small tomato, seeded and chopped
1 teaspoon Tabasco sauce
¼ cup (2 oz.) dry white wine
1 bay leaf
  Salt to taste
  Freshly ground pepper
2 tablespoons chopped pimento for garnish

In a large saucepan, bring the water to a boil. Add the lima beans and cook over medium heat until just tender. Drain and remove to a warm bowl.

In a large skillet, heat the olive oil and sauté the chorizo, tomato, Tabasco sauce, wine, bay leaf, salt, and pepper for about 3 minutes. Add the lima beans and mix well with the sauce. Cover and cook over low heat for about 5—10 minutes or until the beans are soft. Discard bay leaf. Transfer the beans to a serving bowl and garnish with the chopped pimento.

SAUTÉED GARLIC AND PIMENTOS
AJO Y PIMIENTOS SALTEADOS

Sometimes a bright, spicy small vegetable dish can make a meal. This is one of those dishes. I recommend large, white garlic and either imported or home-cooked roasted pimentos. This fascinating dish is easy to prepare in five minutes. Yes, five minutes, maybe less.

SERVES 4

3 tablespoons olive oil
2 cloves garlic, peeled and mashed
4 whole canned or roasted peeled pimentos cut in
    1-inch slices
  Salt to taste
  Freshly ground pepper
10 small stuffed olives for garnish

In a large skillet, heat the olive oil over medium-high heat and sauté the garlic and pimentos, shaking the pan briskly, until the pimentos start to darken.

Remove the pimentos to a serving platter, sprinkle with salt and pepper, and garnish with the olives.

Salads / Ensaladas

POTATO SALAD VALENCIA STYLE
PATATAS A LA VALENCIANA

Valencia is orange country. The sweetest orange variety is the Valencia. Typically Valencian, this recipe is an unusual combination of fresh ingredients that creates a potato salad very different from all the potato salads you've ever eaten.

SERVES 4

    2   tangerines, peeled and separated into sections
    3   thin slices red onion
   10   small new potatoes, whole, scrubbed, and steamed
         until fork-tender

DRESSING
    4   tablespoons orange juice
   ½   teaspoon brandy
    1   tablespoon grated Parmesan
    2   tablespoons chopped pimento
         Salt to taste
         Freshly ground pepper
   ½   cup olive oil

Place the tangerines, onions, and potatoes in a large salad bowl.

In a food processor or blender, combine the orange juice, brandy, Parmesan, pimento, salt, pepper, and olive oil. Blend until smooth. Pour the dressing over the salad and mix well. Serve at room temperature.

PIMENTO AND GREEN PEPPER SALAD
ENSALADA DE PIMIENTO

This authentic Spanish salad will probably be the easiest salad you ever prepared. All the ingredients come ready to use except the green pepper and parsley. And how hard can they be . . . chop, chop, chop, chop . . . you know what I mean.

SERVES 4

2 canned whole pimentos, cut in 1-inch slices
2 medium green bell peppers, seeded and cut in 1-inch slices
4 thin slices red onion
¼ cup raisins, soaked in water and drained
8 small stuffed green olives
½ teaspoon dry oregano
Salt to taste
Freshly ground pepper
¼ cup virgin olive oil
4 sprigs parsley for garnish
Grated Parmesan (optional)

Place all ingredients (except parsley and Parmesan) in a salad bowl and mix well. Refrigerate for about 2 hours before serving. Serve on individual salad plates and garnish with a sprig of parsley. Sprinkle on grated cheese if desired.

Soups / Sopas

COLLARD GREENS SOUP
SOPA DE ACELGAS

I call this recipe the "Prince and Pauper" soup. It combines the world's most inexpensive vegetable with the world's most expensive spice. It is also highly nutritious, and when served with hot crunchy bread it is a grande meal. Rich or poor, you'll love it.

4   cups water
6   cups chicken broth
1   cup (8 oz.) dry white wine
½   teaspoon crumbled saffron
½   teaspoon paprika
½   cup chopped onion
    Salt to taste
    Freshly ground pepper
2   medium carrots, peeled and cut in ½-inch rounds
1   pound fresh collard greens, stems removed, coarsely
        chopped
3   tablespoons chopped fresh cilantro
1¼ cups uncooked rice

In a large casserole, combine the water, broth, wine, saffron, paprika, onion, salt, and pepper and bring to a boil. Add the carrots, greens, and cilantro and cook uncovered over low heat for about 25 minutes. Add the rice and check for seasoning. Cover and cook over low heat for about 20 minutes or until the rice is done. Serve in individual soup bowls and garnish with a sprig of parsley.

Rice / Arrozes

SEAFOOD-FLAVORED RICE
ARROZ A BANDA

This is one of the most traditional recipes of Levante. Every home has a plentiful supply of fish broth from all the seafood available in the region. The combination of spices, vegetables, rice, and broth fills this dish with many flavors from the farm and the sea.

4   cloves garnish, peeled, 2 whole, 2 chopped
1   dried sweet red pepper "New Mexico style," stem
        and seeds removed
½   teaspoon salt

¼ teaspoon freshly ground pepper
2 tablespoons chopped flat parsley
½ teaspoon crumbled saffron
1 cup clam broth
½ cup olive oil
2 cloves garlic, chopped
1 tomato, finely chopped
½ cup (4 oz.) dry white wine
2½ cups fish broth
    Salt to taste
    Freshly ground black pepper to taste
2 cups short-grain rice

In a food processor or blender, mix the 2 whole cloves of garlic, red pepper, salt, black pepper, parsley, saffron, and clam broth. Blend until smooth.

In a large casserole, heat the oil and sauté the chopped garlic and the tomato for about 2 minutes. Add the wine, fish broth, the blender mixture, salt, and pepper. Bring to a boil over high heat.

Add the rice and stir well.

Cook uncovered over medium-high heat for about 20 minutes or until the rice is semi-dry. Cover and cook over low heat for about 20 minutes more or until the rice is done. Turn the rice with a fork from bottom to top, cover, and continue cooking for 5 more minutes. Transfer the rice to a large serving bowl.

Serve with Alioli Sauce (see recipe for Grilled Beef with Garlic Mayonnaise).

CHICKEN AND RICE
ARROZ CON POLLO

Arroz con Pollo is as basic as you can get in Spanish cuisine. Like hamburgers in America, you'll find chicken and rice everywhere in Spain. This recipe, which I was given by my grandmother, will introduce you to the very best version I've ever eaten. And I've eaten plenty of Arroz con Pollo.

SERVES 4

3 pounds chicken, cut in small serving pieces
Salt and pepper to taste
6 tablespoons olive oil
2 green bell peppers, seeded and chopped
1 onion, chopped
4 cloves garlic, crushed
2 tablespoons minced fresh cilantro
2 fresh tomatoes, peeled and chopped
2 canned or roasted peeled fresh pimentos
3 tablespoons paprika
½ teaspoon crumbled saffron
3½ cups chicken broth
½ cup (4 oz.) dry white wine
2 cups uncooked rice
1 tablespoon minced parsley for garnish
4 orange slices for garnish

Sprinkle the chicken pieces with salt and pepper and set aside. In a large casserole, heat the oil and sauté the chicken until golden on all sides. Remove chicken to a warm platter. Add the green peppers, onion, garlic, and cilantro and sauté until onion is soft. Add the tomatoes and pimentos and cook, uncovered, for 10 minutes more. Add the paprika, saffron, broth, wine, salt, and pepper and bring to a boil. Add the rice and cook over medium-high heat, uncovered, for about 20 minutes, stirring until rice is semi-dry but some liquid remains.

Bury the chicken in the rice. Cover and cook over low heat for about 20 minutes. Turn the rice and chicken over with a fork from bottom to top; cover and simmer for another 10 minutes. Transfer rice and chicken to a serving platter and garnish with the parsley and the orange slices.

Serve this dish with a Pimento and Green Pepper Salad.

RICE WITH SHRIMP AND SCALLOPS
ARROZ AL CALDERO

The last time I visited Florida, I experienced this beautiful Rice with Shrimp and Scallops dish at Ramiro's Restaurant in Coral Gables. I was informed that the recipe originated in Valencia. Of course, I have incorporated my own touch—dried sweet red pepper. And why not? This robust, multiflavored dish stands alone at any meal.

SERVES 4

6	tablespoons olive oil
8	large shrimp, shelled
6	cloves garlic, mashed
4	tablespoons chopped flat parsley
2	dried sweet red peppers "New Mexico style," stem and seeds removed, chopped
1	canned or roasted, peeled fresh pimento, chopped
3½	cups fish broth
½	cup (4 oz.) dry white wine
2	cups short-grain rice
	Salt to taste
	Freshly ground pepper
1½	pounds fresh large scallops
2	tablespoons chopped pimento for garnish
1	tablespoon chopped parsley for garnish

In a large casserole, heat the oil and sauté the shrimp until it starts to turn pink. Remove to a warm platter. Add the garlic, parsley, red peppers, and pimento and sauté for about 3 minutes, shaking the pan briskly. Add the broth and wine and bring to a boil. Add the rice, salt, and pepper and mix well. Cook, uncovered, over medium heat until rice is semi-dry but some liquid remains.

Bury the reserved shrimp and the scallops in the rice. Cover and cook over low heat for about 20 minutes. Uncover and turn the rice and seafood over with a fork from bottom to top. Cover and simmer for another 10 minutes. Transfer the rice to a serving platter and garnish with the chopped pimento and chopped parsley.

CHICKEN AND SHELLFISH RICE
PAELLA VALENCIANA

This dish is Spain. It took centuries of history to create this recipe, the flagship of all Spanish dishes. It took the Romans to invent the two-handled, shallow metal pan called patella. *(The name* paella *refers to the pan, not the ingredients.) Then it took the Arabs to perfect the Roman irrigation system that created wetlands where rice was first introduced to Europe. The Arabs also introduced saffron, basic to all paellas. There are as many paella recipes as there are cooks. Everything and anything goes. Paella originated in Valencia, where the rice first grew and where seafood, vegetables, fowl, and saffron abounded. We Spanish are so proud of this dish we want to share it with you. We believe in giving and receiving. So if you create a paella recipe you're proud of, please share it with me.* Muchas gracias.

SERVES 6 – 8

¼	cup olive oil
1½	pounds chicken, cut in small serving pieces and sprinkled with salt and pepper
10	large shrimp, shelled
2	lobster tails, split lengthwise
¼	pound chorizo, cut in ½-inch slices
¼	pound diced serrano or prosciutto ham
6	cloves garlic, peeled and mashed
1	medium onion, peeled and chopped
3	tablespoons chopped fresh cilantro
2	bay leaves, crumbled
2	whole roasted pimentos, diced
½	cup (4 oz.) dry white wine
3½	cups chicken broth
½	teaspoon crumbled saffron
1	cup frozen peas
	Salt to taste
	Freshly ground pepper
2	cups short-grain rice
6	small clams, well scrubbed
6	medium mussels, well scrubbed
4	lemon slices for garnish

4   orange slices for garnish
8   stuffed olives for garnish
2   tablespoons chopped parsley for garnish

In a large paella pan (or large casserole), heat the oil and sauté the chicken until golden on all sides. Remove to a warm platter. In the same pan, sauté the shrimp and lobster until they just turn pink. Remove to a warm platter. Add the chorizo, ham, garlic, onion, cilantro, bay leaves, and pimentos and sauté until onion is soft.

Add the wine, broth, saffron, peas, salt, and pepper and bring to a boil. Add the rice and mix well. Cook, uncovered, over medium heat until rice is semi-dry but some liquid remains. Bury the chicken and shrimp in the rice. Push the clams and mussels into the rice with the hinge-end facing down. Arrange the lobster tails in the center of the paella dish.

Bake in a 325°F preheated oven for about 15 minutes. Remove from the oven and let sit for about 10 minutes. Garnish with the lemon and orange slices and olives and sprinkle with the chopped parsley.

RICE WITH CHORIZO
ARROZ CON CHORIZO

Take lean meat, paprika, garlic, and olive oil. Grind and mix well. Hang in the Spanish sunshine. ¡Ole! Chorizo, the famous Spanish sausage. The sizzle will whet your appetite. The final dish will satisfy it.

SERVES 4

3   tablespoons olive oil
2   large cloves garlic, mashed
1   medium onion, peeled and chopped
2   chorizos cut in ½-inch rounds
¼   cup chopped fresh cilantro
¼   cup canned crushed tomatoes
1   tablespoon tomato paste
3   cups chicken broth
1½   cups short-grain rice
       Salt to taste
8   small stuffed olives for garnish
3   orange slices for garnish

In a medium casserole (3 quarts), heat the oil and sauté garlic, onion, and chorizo for about 3 minutes or until the onion is soft. Add 3 tablespoons of the cilantro, the tomatoes, and the tomato paste and cook over high heat for about a minute. Add the broth and continue cooking until broth comes to a boil. Add the rice and salt to taste. Cook for about 10 minutes or until the rice is semi-dry but some liquid remains. Cover and cook over low heat for about 20 minutes or until the rice is dry.

Turn the rice from bottom to top with a fork and continue cooking, covered, for about 10 more minutes.

Transfer the rice to a serving platter and garnish with the olives, orange slices, and the rest of the cilantro.

Serve with green, leafy vegetables like kale, collards, or escarole.

RICE WITH VEGETABLES
PAELLA DE VEGETABLES

I don't want to forget my vegetarian friends. I have plenty, you know. This is a dish from the garden. Pick a wide variety of vegetables from your own garden, the produce store, or the frozen foods case. You can substitute water for the chicken broth, but take this tip: Before adding the water to the rice, add ½ teaspoon ground cumin to the water, mix and let sit for about 10 minutes. You'll enjoy this meal for its flavor, its nutrition, and its peace of mind. Paz y amor.

SERVES 4

5	tablespoons olive oil
4	cloves garlic, mashed
1	large onion, chopped
6	tablespoons chopped fresh cilantro
1	pimento (canned), chopped
½	cup canned crushed tomatoes
2	medium carrots, scraped and thinly sliced
4	cups chicken broth or water
½	teaspoon crumbled saffron
	Salt to taste
2	cups uncooked rice
½	pound small zucchini, cut in ½-inch rounds
½	pound small yellow squash, cut in ½-inch rounds
½	cup frozen peas

2   tablespoons chopped cilantro for garnish
4   orange slices for garnish

   In a large paella pan, heat the oil and sauté the garlic, onion, 6 tablespoons cilantro, pimento, tomato, and carrots for about 5 minutes, shaking the pan briskly. Add the broth or water, saffron, and salt to taste and bring to a boil. Add rice and mix well. Cook over medium heat for about 20 minutes or until the rice is semi-dry but some liquid remains. Bury the zucchini, yellow squash, and peas in the rice and bake in a 325°F preheated oven for about 15 minutes or until the liquid has evaporated. Remove and let sit for about 10 minutes.
   Garnish with the remaining cilantro and the orange slices.

Fish / Pescado

ORANGE BASS
MERO A LA NARANJA

Once again the sweet Valencia orange helps create another marvelous dish from Levante. The orange aroma and sweet citrus taste give the bass a succulence and tang not usually found in fish recipes.

SERVES 4

4   bass fillets (about 8 oz. each)
     Salt to taste
     Freshly ground pepper
     Olive oil to moisten
1   large orange, cut in half
8   thin orange slices for garnish

   Sprinkle the fish with salt, pepper, and olive oil on both sides.
   Place the fish in an oiled or buttered baking pan. Squeeze the juice of the orange over the fillets and bake in a 350°F preheated oven for about 20 minutes or until the fish is done. Transfer the fish to a serving platter and garnish with the orange slices.
   Serve with one of my rice recipes, baked potato, or pasta. Baby carrots make an excellent vegetable side dish.

STRIPED BASS IN WALNUT SAUCE
LUBINA A LA VALENCIANA

In this rare recipe, the unusual combination of seafood and walnuts produces an exotic and surprising taste. It is also a high-protein meal with a minimum of fat. Salud.

SERVES 4

¼   cup ground walnuts
6   cloves garlic, peeled
5   tablespoons chopped flat parsley
¼   teaspoon paprika
1½   cups fish broth
     Salt to taste
     Freshly ground pepper
3   tablespoons olive oil
4   striped bass fillets (about 6 oz. each)
4   walnuts, coarsely chopped, for garnish

In a food processor or blender, mix the ground walnuts, garlic, parsley, paprika, broth, salt, and pepper and blend until smooth.

In a large skillet, heat the oil and sauté the fish for about 2 minutes on each side. Pour the blender mixture over the fish. Cover and cook over low heat for about 20 minutes or until the fish is done.

Transfer the fish to a serving platter and pour the sauce over it. Garnish with the chopped walnuts and serve hot.

Serve with Cauliflower Muleteer Style and a baked potato.

Desserts / Postres

ORANGES CARAMELADE
NARANJAS A LA VALENCIANA

This is a typical dessert of Valencia. Why? Oranges! The recipe was given to me by a dear friend residing in Sueca, Levante, and the wide variety of citrus fruits gives you a different flavor in every spoonful. The tartness of the citrus and the sweet caramel create a true taste sensation.

SERVES 4

2   tangerines, mandarins, clementines, or navel oranges,
     peeled and separated into sections
1   cup sugar
3   tablespoons water
1   teaspoon Grand Marnier liqueur

Pat dry the orange sections with paper towel. On a greased cookie sheet, place the orange sections in a row with rounded side facing down.

In a small saucepan, combine the sugar, water, and liqueur. Melt over low heat, mixing slowly with a fork until sugar is lightly carmelized. Working quickly, pour the caramel over the orange sections to coat well. Let cool at room temperature. When cool, separate each segment. Transfer to a serving bowl and refrigerate.

Serve with black coffee.

The Old Roman Bridge at Ronda

ANDALUCÍA

Andalucía is gypsies. Andalucía is vineyards stretching from the southern coast northward to the mountains. Andalucía is the birthplace of bullfights. Andalucía is seaports and cities whose names reflect the history of Spain from its primal origins to its present-day place as an international commercial and cultural center. Long before the Romans came with their laws, political structures, road builders, and artists, Andalucía was host to the Greeks and Phoenicians who developed the fertile lands, the abundant southern shores, and the friendly harbors for commerce, agriculture, and shipping. The great romantic cities of Cádiz, Seville, Córdoba, Málaga, and Granada were thriving in the sixth and seventh centuries. These cities became jewels in the crowns of the Moorish caliphs who came during the eighth century and added a thick layer of Muslim culture that still exists today in the language, the architecture, the bloodlines, and the cuisine of Andalucía. Among their enormous contributions, the Moorish visitors created the Great Mosque in Córdoba and the Alhambra in Granada with its interior gardens and whispering ponds. Seville became the center of artistic splendor and intellectual thought as the Arab world developed the natural resources of Spain's southernmost region into a magnificent and exciting civilization.

For over three hundred years the Arab world refined and defined the raw beauty and energy of the Andalucían region into a harmonious and provident culture. Great thinkers and commercial planners joined with architects, farmers, craftsmen, and artists to create a society that was an example to the Western world.

Even after the reconquest of Spain and the last Arab ruler surrendered to the combined forces of Spanish military crusaders and Christian kings, Andalucía was left with deep roots in basic civilization: family, home, loyalty, kinship, and history. The dark-skinned, romantic

21

Andalucians found themselves rich in natural resources and became a society of craftsmen, artisans, cattle ranchers and shepherds, field hands, and small merchants. The southern sun blessed the vineyards, and the English came and developed the vast international wine industry that today sends thousands and thousands of barrels of sherry and wine all over the world from Cádiz—the same port that launched Columbus into the New World.

The Greek, Phoenician, Arab, French, and English invaders came to Andalucía, not to destroy it, but to love it and leave the best of their cultures to flourish in this land that seems to nourish all living things. The seacoast yields fish and shellfish in an endless abundance. The rich soil provides vegetables and fruits of all descriptions. Spices and fresh herbs grow profusely with variety and intensity. These gifts of the earth and sea, the vine and the tree, combined with domestic and wild animal life, inspired the chefs of all cultures to highly imaginative effort in the preparation and presentation of beautiful food. The recipes of the region are filled with seafood and meat combinations; fruits in soup; tomatoes prepared in endless variety; colorful, vibrant salads; vegetables accompanied by natural fresh herbs; and irresistible little appetizers called tapas, which represent the imagination, the history, and the abundance of Andalucía.

TAPAS OF ANDALUCÍA

Tapas were originally created in Andalucía in the area of Jerez. *Tapa* comes from the word *tapar*, which literally means "to cover." The name was given to the complimentary slices of bread and cheese (or dried ham or sausage) that were placed over the wineglasses served to patrons of the numerous cantinas in the region. Some say the purpose of the tapa was to keep flies out of the sweet sherry or to protect the wine from dust. It is also true that the salty sausage, ham, cheese, and bread added to the thirst of the Andalucían horsemen and field workers, no doubt increasing the consumption of sherry and wine.

Today tapas can be any delicious combination of finger food presented colorfully and simply. Tapas have become internationally recognized as a delightful and civilized beginning to any meal.

SHERRY, BRANDY, AND WINES OF ANDALUCÍA

Long before the Romans came, Andalucía was making wine. In the western portion of the region lies Jerez de la Frontera. From early spring until the September harvest, life here revolves around the growing, tending, and picking of the grapes. Between the harvest and the next spring, the grapes are transformed into some of the world's finest wines and spirits. Sherries, brandies, and wines of all colors and character are produced in this land of fertile soils and perfect sunlight.

Giant bodegas of classic design and architecture house barrel upon barrel in row upon row of aging sherries. They are continuously blended from old to new to create the consistent quality and flavor demanded of a true sherry.

Originally simply called Jerez, these liquors became immensely popular with the British. (At one point in 1587 Sir Francis Drake pirated over three thousand barrels of sherry and sailed them home to England.) The British corruption of the Spanish word *Jerez* became *sherris* and ultimately the present form of *sherry*. This British passion for sherry brought to Andalucía many merchants who created the bodegas and labels that still carry many English names although now mostly Spanish owned. The British wine merchants adopted Andalucía as their new home, intermarried, and added to the rich culture that is Spain.

Jerez produces almost as much brandy, a distilled product that is sweeter and darker than sherry. Andalucían brandies rival the best brandies of the world and are preferred by Spaniards to any cognac at any price.

Often underestimated, it is the wines of Andalucía that offer the greatest surprise and delight. They are fresh and alive with a full range of flavors from the pale, straw-colored, fragrant finos to the very sweet, sun-filled dark ruby Ximenez. There are the classic, sweet Málaga wines with many characteristics, including the gentle Lagrima, which is never mechanically pressed. The juice is collected from natural flow only. Many of these Málaga wines are created in small bodegas that carefully blend and bottle special wines in small quantities. The availability of fine Spanish wines is ever-increasing, with some seventy firms shipping their labels from the port of Cádiz alone. The companion wine to your perfect Spanish meal awaits your choosing and will add a classic taste to your dining pleasure.

Appetizers / Tapas

MUSHROOMS WITH GARLIC
SETAS CON AJO

This particular dish is for garlic lovers. In addition to its special flavor, garlic is healthy, and I highly recommend its use. These mushroom garlic tapas are easy to prepare, and with a touch of cilantro are muy delicioso.

SERVES 4

¼	cup olive oil
4	cloves garlic, mashed
1 ½	tablespoons flour
1	cup chicken broth
½	teaspoon crushed red pepper
3	tablespoons chopped fresh cilantro
	Salt to taste
½	pound mushrooms, stems removed
3	tablespoons chopped parsley for garnish

Heat 2 tablespoons of the olive oil in a large skillet and sauté the garlic for about 2 minutes. Add the flour and mix well. Add the broth, crushed pepper, cilantro, and salt. Cook over medium heat for about 10 minutes, uncovered.

Meanwhile, in a separate large skillet sauté the mushrooms in the rest of the olive oil until lightly colored.

Transfer the mushrooms to the sauce, mix well, cover, and cook over low heat for about 10 minutes. Transfer the mixture to a deep serving platter and sprinkle with the chopped parsley.

HAM AND PORK ROLLS
FRITILLAS AL MORO

The Moors were in Spain for more than 700 years, and these Al Moro tapas reflect that legacy. Even though I have made some changes from the original, the recipe is truly Spanish/Moorish. If lower fat is a consideration, I recommend you substitute chicken for the pork.

SERVES 4

¼   cup olive oil
    Salt to taste
    Freshly ground pepper
½   teaspoon paprika
¾   pound pork loin, cut into 12 1-inch cubes
6   slices bacon, cut in half
2   tablespoons chopped parsley for garnish

In a medium bowl, combine the oil, salt, pepper, and paprika and mix well. Add the pork to the marinade, coat well, and set aside for about 15 minutes.

Wrap half a slice of bacon around each pork cube and secure with a toothpick.

Place the wrapped pork cubes in a broiler pan and broil, turning once, for about 10 minutes or until the meat is done. Remove to a serving platter and sprinkle with the parsley.

CARROTS WITH SHERRY WINE
ZANAHORIAS AL JEREZ

Cooking with sherry, or Jerez, is typically Andalucían. If you like carrots, you will love the way the Andalucíans prepare them.

SERVES 4

2½ pounds thin carrots, cut in 1-inch thick rounds
3   tablespoons chopped parsley for garnish

DRESSING
4   cloves garlic, mashed
1   tablespoon dried oregano

¼   teaspoon cumin
¼   teaspoon crushed red pepper
2   teaspoons chopped fresh cilantro
1½   tablespoons sherry wine vinegar
2   tablespoons sherry wine
     Salt to taste
     Freshly ground pepper
½   cup olive oil

Steam the carrots until tender, about 10 minutes. Drain and place in a serving bowl. In a food processor or blender, add the garlic, oregano, cumin, crushed red pepper, cilantro, vinegar, wine, salt, and pepper. Blend until a paste is formed. With the motor running, add the oil in a thin stream until mixture is a smooth consistency. Pour the dressing over the carrots and sprinkle with parsley.

SCALLOP FRITTERS
BUÑUELOS DE VIEIRAS

Golden, crispy, and very flavorful, these unusual Andalucian tapas make a great snack or side dish as well as an interesting appetizer. If you have a nonstick pan, you can reduce the frying oil to the amount you normally use for pancakes.

SERVES 4

¼   cup olive oil
2   cloves garlic, mashed
¼   cup finely chopped onion
¼   teaspoon paprika
½   teaspoon oregano
2   tablespoons minced fresh cilantro
¼   cup flour
10   tablespoons water
½   teaspoon baking powder
¼   pound small sea scallops, finely chopped
     Salt to taste
     Oil for frying

In a medium skillet, heat the 4 tablespoons of oil and sauté the garlic, onion, paprika, oregano, and cilantro until onion is soft.

Meantime, in a medium bowl mix the flour, water, baking powder, the mixture from the skillet, the scallops, and salt until very smooth and thick.

Wipe off the skillet, add frying oil to a depth of ½ to 1 inch, and heat until very hot. Add the batter, one tablespoon at a time, to form 3-inch "pancakes." Fry until golden and crispy. Drain over paper towels and serve warm.

PORK SHISH KABOB
PINCHO ARABE

The name shish kabob *comes from the Arab word* kababah, *which means "cut into cubes." The Moorish technique combined with Spanish flavor creates a classic Spanish/Moorish recipe. If low fat is a concern, substitute chicken or turkey chunks for the pork.*

SERVES 4

MARINADE
2	cloves garlic, peeled
4	tablespoons chopped onion
1	teaspoon ground cumin
½	teaspoon crushed red pepper
3	tablespoons chopped fresh cilantro
¼	cup water
	Salt to taste
½	cup olive oil
1	pound lean pork, cut in 1-inch cubes
4–6	cherry tomatoes
4–6	slices bread

In a food processor or blender, mix all ingredients except the olive oil, pork, tomatoes, and bread. With the motor running, add the oil in a thin stream until the mixture is smooth.

Place the meat in a bowl and pour the marinade over it to coat it well. Set aside, covered, in refrigerator, for about 2 hours.

Thread the pork cubes on 4 to 6 small skewers. Top each skewer with a tomato.

Cook the kabobs over an outside barbecue or under a broiler, basting frequently with the reserved marinade, until meat is tender. Place the kabobs over the slices of bread and serve.

Vegetables / Legumbres

LIMA BEANS AND SAFFRON
HABAS AL MORO

Lima beans are a delicious favorite in Andalucía. Saffron is the most expensive spice in the world. But have no fear, you only need a pinch. The results are maravilloso.

SERVES 4

1	cup chicken broth
½	teaspoon crumbled saffron
1	pound fresh lima beans, or 1 package (10 oz.) frozen
3	cloves garlic
1	small onion, peeled and chopped
3	tablespoons chopped fresh cilantro
½	cup canned crushed tomatoes
¼	teaspoon cumin
	Salt to taste
	Freshly ground pepper
3	tablespoons olive oil
2	sprigs parsley for garnish

In a large skillet, combine the broth, saffron, and lima beans and bring to a boil. Cover and steam over low heat for about 10 minutes.

Meanwhile, in a food processor or blender add the garlic, onion, cilantro, tomato, cumin, salt, and pepper and mix until smooth. With the motor running, add the oil in a thin stream.

Pour the mixture from the blender over the beans and mix well. Continue cooking for about 10 more minutes or until the beans are soft. Transfer the mixture to a serving platter and garnish with the parsley.

I recommend you serve this dish with White Rice and Sherry or as a vegetable companion to red meats and gravy.

MUSHROOMS IN SHERRY SAUCE
SETAS AL JEREZ

Nobody cooks with sherry better than the Spanish; they invented it. This recipe combines the subtle flavor of mushrooms with the dramatic smooth taste of a Spanish sherry. It will become one of your favorites.

SERVES 4

¼   cup olive oil
¼   cup chopped onions
1   pound small mushrooms, washed, stems trimmed
2   teaspoons flour
2   tablespoons chopped fresh cilantro
¼   cup chicken broth
¼   cup (2 oz.) dry sherry
¼   teaspoon lemon juice
    Salt to taste
    Freshly ground pepper
6   lemon slices for garnish

In a large skillet, heat the oil and sauté the onion and mushrooms for about 5 minutes. Remove mushrooms and onion to a serving platter.

In the same skillet, add the flour and mix well until smooth. Add the cilantro, broth, sherry, lemon juice, salt, and pepper and cook over low heat for about 6–8 minutes. Pour the mixture over the mushrooms and garnish with lemon slices.

Serve this mushroom dish ladled over a filet mignon, steak, or boneless breast of chicken.

CAULIFLOWER MULETEER STYLE
COLIFLOR AL ARRIERO

On a trip to Chicago I had the opportunity to visit one of the most popular Spanish restaurants in that city, Cafe Ba-Ba-Reeba. Their presentation of tapas was outstanding, especially this traditional Andalucian dish.

SERVES 4

1   head medium cauliflower, broken into florets
4   cloves garlic, peeled
3   tablespoons chopped onion
2   tablespoons chopped flat parsley
2   tablespoons canned crushed tomatoes
¼   cup chicken broth
2   tablespoons sherry wine vinegar
½   teaspoon dried sweet basil (1 tablespoon chopped fresh basil)
½   tablespoon paprika
    Salt to taste
6   tablespoons virgin olive oil

In a medium saucepan, steam the cauliflower in salted water; drain. Transfer the cauliflower to a serving platter and keep warm.

In a food processor or blender, add the garlic, onion, parsley, tomatoes, broth, vinegar, basil, paprika, and salt and blend until smooth. With the motor running, add the oil slowly in a smooth stream.

Transfer the mixture to the medium saucepan, cover, and cook over low heat for about 10 minutes, stirring occasionally. Pour the mixture over the cauliflower and serve hot.

A nice way to enjoy this recipe is to mix it with your favorite pasta.

LIMA BEANS AND SCALLIONS
HABAS A LA MÁLAGA

Chorizo is a dried lean sausage spiced with paprika and found everywhere in Spain. Each region produces its own version, and one of the best comes from Andalucía. Cooked with fresh or frozen lima beans, it becomes a nutritious and satisfying side dish. If you cannot find chorizo, substitute sweet or hot dried Italian sausage.

SERVES 4

3   tablespoons olive oil
3   cloves garlic, chopped
1   scallion, chopped
4   tablespoons chopped chorizo
1½ pounds fresh baby lima beans (24 oz. frozen)
5   tablespoons dry white wine

Salt to taste
Freshly ground pepper
2   tablespoons chopped parsley for garnish

In a large skillet, heat the olive oil and sauté the garlic, scallion, and chorizo until the sausage starts to sizzle. Add the lima beans, wine, salt, and pepper and mix well. Cover and cook over low heat for about 10–15 minutes or until the beans are soft. Transfer to a serving platter and garnish with the chopped parsley.

Serve this dish with a soup for a light but delicious meal.

PEAS AND ONIONS WITH HAM
GUISANTES ESTILO ANDALUCÍA

Peas are highly nutritious, and when picked early and tiny they are sugary-sweet. The combination of sharp pearl onions and the spicy taste of serrano or prosciutto makes an interesting and unusual dish with complex flavors. I am especially fond of this dish because it comes from my grandmother's kitchen.

SERVES 4

3   tablespoons olive oil
20   tiny pearl onions, peeled
5   tablespoons minced serrano or prosciutto ham
1   tablespoon chopped chorizo
1   tablespoon chopped fresh cilantro
2   cups fresh or frozen peas
     Salt to taste
     Freshly ground pepper
½   chopped pimento for garnish

In a large skillet, heat the oil and sauté the onion for about 3 minutes. Add the ham and sausage and cook over medium-high heat, shaking the skillet briskly for about a minute. Add the cilantro, peas, salt, and pepper and mix well. Cover and cook over low heat for about 10 minutes or until the peas are soft. Transfer the mixture to a serving platter and garnish with the chopped pimento.

Serve this hearty vegetable dish with hot crunchy bread. Ummmmm . . . muy bueno.

Salads / Ensaladas

SUMMER TUNA SALAD ANDALUCÍA STYLE
ENSALADILLA DE ATÚN

For those caliente *days I highly recommend this Costa del Sol salad. The combination of greens, tuna, Manchego or Parmesan cheese, and olive oil dressing is a light but* muy delicioso *hot-weather meal. If low fat is a factor, substitute a low-fat or skim-milk cheese.*

SERVES 4

1	large carrot, peeled and sliced
1	medium green bell pepper, seeded and finely diced
1	medium red bell pepper, seeded and finely diced
1	small onion, finely sliced
1	stalk celery, coarsely chopped
2	large tomatoes, seeded and diced
2	scallions, coarsely chopped (green parts only)
3	cans (7 oz. each) chunk white tuna, drained

DRESSING
½	cup virgin olive oil
3	tablespoons sherry wine vinegar
½	tablespoon dried oregano
½	teaspoon granulated garlic (1 large clove peeled and mashed)
1	tablespoon grated Manchego or Parmesan cheese
	Salt to taste
	Freshly ground pepper

In a large bowl, combine all the vegetable ingredients and the tuna. Mix well.

In a jar with a lid, combine all the dressing ingredients and shake well.

Pour the dressing over the vegetables and tuna and toss well. Chill before serving.

ESCAROLE WITH OLIVES AND CHEESE
ENSALADA ESTÍLO MORO

If you think salads are bland and boring, this Moorish/Spanish recipe will perk up your spirits. The sharp escarole with tangy olives and a sharp blue-veined Cabrales cheese dressed with sherry vinegar and olive oil will make you ask for more salad, por favor.

SERVES 4

DRESSING

1	cup canned crushed tomatoes
½	teaspoon ground cumin
2	cloves garlic, crushed
2	tablespoons chopped onion
2	tablespoons sherry wine vinegar
¼	teaspoon dried crushed marjoram leaves
	Salt to taste
	Freshly ground pepper
¼	cup virgin olive oil

1	head escarole, washed thoroughly and cut up coarsely
4	teaspoons grated Manchego or crumbled Cabrales cheese
16	stuffed green olives

In a food processor or blender, add the tomatoes, cumin, garlic, onion, vinegar, marjoram, salt, and pepper. Blend until smooth. With the motor running, add the oil in a thin stream.

Arrange the escarole in individual salad bowls and pour some of the dressing over each one. Top with grated cheese and the olives.

Soups / Sopas

GAZPACHO CÓRDOBA STYLE
GAZPACHO DE CÓRDOBA

There are as many gazpacho recipes as there are Spanish cooks. This recipe comes from my dearest aunt America, who sent me the recipe from her home in San Andres. Her "secret" ingredient is the marjoram. If a meatless or low-fat dish is desirable, eliminate the serrano ham.

SERVES 4

4	cups canned, peeled, crushed tomatoes
1	egg yolk
2	cloves garlic, minced
1	tablespoon chopped onion
4	ounces white bread (or two slices), crusts removed
¼	teaspoon crushed marjoram leaves
2	tablespoons sherry wine vinegar
	Salt to taste
	Freshly ground pepper
6	tablespoons virgin olive oil
3	tablespoons chopped fresh cilantro for garnish
2	ounces serrano or prosciutto ham, thinly sliced and chopped, for garnish

In a food processor or blender, add all the ingredients, a little at a time, except the olive oil and the garnish and blend until smooth. While the motor is running, add the olive oil in a thin stream. Blend well. Strain the mixture through a wire strainer.

Pour the soup into individual soup bowls and refrigerate for about 1 hour or longer. Garnish with the ham and the cilantro and serve.

COLD TOMATO AND VEGETABLE SOUP
GAZPACHO ANDALUZ

This gazpacho variation comes from Doña Felicita García de Perez, my grandmother. It is a classic for sure. The combination of so many bits of vegetables, herbs, and spices creates an unusual and interesting soup. Gazpacho, by the way, comes from the Latin word caspa, *which means "bits and pieces."*

SERVES 4 – 6

3   cups canned crushed tomatoes
2   cloves garlic, finely chopped
1   medium green bell pepper, seeded and chopped
¼   teaspoon tarragon
1   small onion, peeled and chopped
1   small cucumber, peeled, seeded, and chopped
¼   cup red wine vinegar
¼   teaspoon dried marjoram leaves
¼   teaspoon dried sweet basil
½   teaspoon sugar
1   cup tomato juice
     Salt to taste
     Freshly ground pepper
     Diced green peppers, tomato, onion, and cucumber
         for garnish
     Seasoned croutons for garnish

In a food processor or blender, add all the ingredients a little at a time (except the garnish) and blend on high speed until the mixture is smooth. Strain the mixture through a medium strainer.

Pour the mixture into individual soup bowls and chill in the refrigerator at least 1 hour before serving.

Garnish with the diced vegetables and croutons and serve this cold gazpacho for a hot summer day.

COLD WHITE GAZPACHO WITH GRAPES
GAZPACHO MALAGUEÑO

Gazpacho is one of the signatures of Spain. On a hot summer day, this fruity Málaga gazpacho will cool you and please you. ¡Viva gazpacho!

SERVES 4

4   cups cold water
4   ounces white bread (or two slices), crusts removed
4   cloves garlic, mashed

2　tablespoons white vinegar
3　tablespoons chopped onion
5　ounces almonds, blanched and chopped, or ¾ cup
¼　teaspoon marjoram leaves
　　Salt to taste
6　tablespoons virgin olive oil
20　seedless grapes for garnish
3　tablespoons chopped parsley for garnish

In a food processor or blender, place all the ingredients, a little at a time, except the olive oil and the garnish. With the motor running, add the olive oil in a thin stream until smooth. Strain the soup through a wide strainer.

Pour the gazpacho into individual soup bowls and refrigerate. Garnish with the grapes and the chopped parsley and serve chilled.

Egg Dishes / Tortillas

BAKED EGGS WITH SAUSAGE AND TOMATOES
HUEVOS A LA FLAMÉNCA

This is one of the original Moorish recipes introduced into Spain. It contains cumin, an Arab spice that enhances the flavor of all the vegetables and the eggs. This unusual and tasty dish will make you dance flamenco.

SERVES 4

3　tablespoons olive oil
¼　pound chopped serrano or prosciutto ham
¼　pound chorizo, chopped
½　teaspoon paprika
2　cloves garlic, mashed
1　medium onion, peeled and chopped
¼　teaspoon cumin
1　canned imported whole pimento, chopped
5　asparagus spears, cut in ½-inch pieces
2　cups canned crushed tomatoes

½ cup chicken broth or water
Salt to taste
Freshly ground pepper
4 eggs, or egg substitute equivalent
3 tablespoons chopped cilantro for garnish

In a large skillet, heat the oil and sauté the ham, chorizo, paprika, garlic, onion, and cumin until onion is soft. Add the pimento, asparagus, tomatoes, broth, salt, and pepper and cook over medium heat for about 10 minutes. Pour the sauce mixture into 4 individual ovenproof crocks. Break one egg into each crock.

Place the crocks in a 400°F oven for about 3–4 minutes or until the egg whites are firm. Garnish with cilantro and serve with hot, crusty bread or salted crackers.

Rice / Arrozes

WHITE RICE AND SHERRY
ARROZ BLANCO AL JEREZ

This dish is one of my originals, flavored with the classic taste of a traditional Spanish sherry. The sherry makes this recipe an authentic Andalucían dish. By now I imagine all the cooks in Andalucía are using my recipes. Buena fortuna.

SERVES 4

3 tablespoons olive oil
1 small onion, peeled and chopped
3 cloves garlic, crushed
3½ cups chicken broth
½ cup dry sherry
2 cups uncooked rice
2 pimentos, chopped
Salt to taste

In a large casserole, heat the oil and sauté the onion and garlic until onion is wilted. Add the broth and wine and bring to a boil. Stir in the rice, pimento, and salt. Continue cooking, stirring occasionally, until rice is semi-dry. Cover and simmer over low heat for about 20 minutes. Turn rice over with a fork from bottom to top and cook (covered) for about 10 minutes more. Serve with your favorite main dish.

Shellfish / Mariscos

SHRIMP AND SAUSAGES IN WHITE SAUCE
GAMBAS Y CHORIZO EN SALSA BLANCA

El Meson Madrid, a restaurant in New Jersey, makes this dish superbly. I have added the sausages for additional flavor and to increase the richness of the dish. You can use the recipe as written or eliminate the sausage for a lighter meal.

SERVES 4

WHITE SAUCE
2	tablespoons sweet butter (or less)
1	clove garlic, mashed
1	tablespoon finely minced onion
2	tablespoons flour
1	teaspoon Dijon-style mustard
½	cup milk
½	cup fish or clam broth
	Salt to taste
	Dash white pepper

3	tablespoons butter (or less)
20	large shrimp, shelled
¼	cup (2 oz.) dry sherry
¼	cup finely chopped chorizo
2	tablespoons minced parsley for garnish

To prepare the white sauce, melt 2 tablespoons butter in a small saucepan and sauté the garlic and onion until onion is soft. Mix in the flour and cook for a minute. Add the mustard, milk, broth, salt, and pepper and stir constantly until sauce is smooth and thick. Remove and set aside.

In a large skillet, heat 3 tablespoons butter and sauté the shrimp and chorizo for about 5 minutes or until the shrimp starts to turn pink. Add the sherry and cook until the sherry evaporates. Transfer the shrimp mixture to a serving platter and pour the white sauce over it. Sprinkle the parsley on top and serve.

This dish is excellent served with Saffron Rice. A glass of Spanish sherry will be the perfect amigo.

LOBSTER IN SHERRY SAUCE
LANGOSTA AL JEREZ

Seafood is king along the southern coast of Andalucía. Tender, sweet lobster simmered in sherry is a classic Spanish dish with extraordinary flavor. It is a full meal with many taste pleasures. Buen apetito.

SERVES 4

4	lobster tails, split lengthwise and crosswise
½	cup butter
2	cloves garlic, mashed
¼	cup chopped onion
2	tablespoons chopped fresh cilantro
4	bay leaves
½	cup (4 oz.) dry sherry
	Salt to taste
	Freshly ground pepper
6	orange slices for garnish

In a large skillet, melt the butter and sauté the lobster until it starts to turn pink. Remove to a warm platter. Add to the skillet the garlic, onion, cilantro, and bay leaves. Cook over medium-high heat for about 5 minutes or until the onion is soft. Add the sherry, salt, and pepper and mix well. Return the lobster to the skillet and continue cooking over medium heat until sherry evaporates. Discard bay leaves. Transfer lobster mixture to a serving platter and garnish with the orange slices.

Serve with any vegetable or one of my favorite Spanish rices.

SHRIMP AND POTATOES WITH GARLIC DRESSING
GAMBAS Y PATATAS ALIÑADAS

The secret to this dish is the dressing. The combination of herbs and spices livens up the shrimp and contrasts with the gentle, sweet taste of the little pink potatoes. It is also very satisfying and rather easy to prepare.

SERVES 4

2	cups water
1	cup (8 oz.) white wine
3	sprigs flat parsley
2	bay leaves
8	peppercorns
	¼-inch piece gingerroot
½	teaspoon salt
20	medium shrimp, shelled
2	pounds very small red or white new potatoes, well scrubbed
¼	cup chopped parsley for garnish

DRESSING

½	teaspoon marjoram leaves
3	cloves garlic, peeled
¼	cup chopped onion
2	tablespoons chopped flat parsley
3	tablespoons wine vinegar
	Salt to taste
	Freshly ground pepper
1	cup virgin olive oil

In a large pot add the water, wine, sprigs of parsley, bay leaves, peppercorns, ginger, and salt and bring to a boil. Reduce the heat to low, add the shrimp, and cook until they turn pink. Remove the shrimp to a serving bowl. Bring the liquid to a second boil and add the potatoes and cook until just soft. Remove the potatoes. Reserve with the shrimp.

In a food processor or blender, place all the ingredients for the dressing except the olive oil. With the motor running, add the oil slowly in a thin stream. Pour dressing over shrimp and potatoes. Toss well, garnish with parsley, and serve at room temperature.

Serve this dish with a crisp green salad.

Fish / Pescado

RED SNAPPER IN SHERRY
PARGO AL JEREZ

When I presented this, one of my favorite dishes on the menu in my restaurant, people loved it. Some say it is the fish. I say it is the sauce. Maybe both!

SERVES 4

4	red snapper fillets (8 oz. each)
	Salt to taste
	Freshly ground pepper
	Flour for dusting
½	cup olive oil
2	cloves garlic, mashed
1	small onion, peeled and chopped
2	tablespoons chopped flat parsley
1	tablespoon flour
½	cup fish broth
½	cup (4 oz.) dry sherry
2	bay leaves
1¾	cups canned crushed tomatoes
4	lemon slices for garnish

Sprinkle the fish with salt and pepper and dust with flour. In a large skillet, heat the oil and sauté the fish until golden on both sides, turning once (be sure fish is done). Remove the fish to a serving platter and keep warm.

In the same skillet, sauté the garlic, onion, and parsley until onion is soft. Add 1 tablespoon flour, broth, sherry, bay leaves, tomatoes, and salt to taste. Mix well until smooth. Cook over medium-high heat for about 10 minutes. Discard bay leaves. Pour the sauce over the fish and garnish with the lemon slices.

This red snapper dish goes well with baked potato or potatoes julienne and broccoli.

BAKED MONKFISH WITH LEEK SAUCE
RAPÉ CON PUERRO

Get your blender ready and heat the oven. This delicious seafood dish is easy to prepare and wonderful to enjoy. ¡Buen provecho!

SERVES 4

4	cloves garlic, peeled
1	medium onion, peeled and coarsely chopped
1	cup finely chopped leek
1½	cups fish broth
½	cup (4 oz.) dry white wine
½	cup (4 oz.) Licor 43
3	tablespoons chopped flat parsley
	Salt to taste
¼	cup olive oil
2	pounds monkfish fillets
6	lemon slices for garnish

In a food processor or blender, mix all ingredients (in a few steps, if necessary) except the olive oil, the garnish, and the fish. With the motor running, add the oil in a thin stream until smooth.

Pour half of the blender mixture in a baking pan and place the fish in the center. Pour the rest of the mixture over the fish and bake in a 350°F preheated oven for about 25 minutes or until the fish is done. Serve in the pan and garnish with the lemon slices.

Serve with White Rice and Sherry or your favorite pasta dish.

CATFISH WITH PEPPERS AND BRANDY
URTA A LA CÁDIZ

This traditional dish comes from Cádiz, in southern Spain near the area of Jerez. It is one of the best dishes in the region's cuisine, and I am excited to bring it to your table.

4   catfish fillets (about ½ lb. each)
     Salt to taste
     Freshly ground pepper
     Flour for dusting
6   tablespoons olive oil
5   cloves garlic, chopped
1   large onion, chopped
1   large green bell pepper, seeded and chopped
½   teaspoon paprika
1   bay leaf, crumbled
2   large tomatoes, seeded and chopped
¾   cup (6 oz.) dry white wine
     Salt to taste
½   cup (4 oz.) brandy
6   orange slices for garnish

Sprinkle the fish with salt and pepper and dust with flour.

In a large skillet, heat 4 tablespoons of the oil and sauté the fish for about a minute on each side; remove to a warm platter. Wipe the skillet and add the remaining oil and sauté the garlic, onions, bell peppers, paprika, and bay leaf until onion is soft. Add the tomato, wine, and salt to taste. Mix well and cook over high heat for about 3 minutes. Return the fish to the skillet and scoop the sauce over the fish. Pour brandy around the fish and flambé (be very careful) until the flames subside.

Cover and cook over low heat for about 15 minutes or until the fish is done. Remove the fish and mixture to a serving platter and garnish with the orange slices.

Serve with a baked potato or over your favorite rice.

BASS IN FENNEL SAUCE
LUBINA CON HINÓJO

If you've never cooked with fennel seed, you're in for a treat. It imparts a subtle anise flavor to the bass. Add the creamy, savory sauce and you're eating al mejor.

SERVES 4

2	cloves garlic
1	small onion, peeled and chopped
¾	cup clam broth
½	cup (4 oz.) dry white wine
6	tablespoons heavy cream or evaporated milk
1	teaspoon finely crushed fennel seeds
½	teaspoon anisette liqueur
	Salt to taste
	Freshly ground pepper
6	tablespoons olive oil
3	tablespoons chopped parsley for garnish

In a food processor or blender (in a few steps if necessary), add the garlic, onion, broth, wine, cream, fennel, liqueur, salt, and pepper and blend well. With the motor running, add the oil in a thin stream until smooth.

Sprinkle the fish with salt and pepper and place in an oiled or buttered baking pan. Pour the blender mixture over the fish and cover the pan with foil. Place the pan in a 350°F preheated oven and bake for about 25 minutes or until fish is done. (Be careful of steam when removing the foil.)

Serve in the baking pan and garnish with the chopped parsley.

Complement this dish with one of my Spanish rice recipes and steamed mixed vegetables.

TUNA WITH ANCHOVY SAUCE
ATÚN CON ANCHOA

This recipe comes from my Aunt Luz Delia. I have made some small changes, which I hope will not upset my aunt. I am sure, however, that she would love the end result. You will, too.

5	cloves garlic, peeled
1	cup canned crushed tomatoes
2	bay leaves, crumbled
1	large pimento (roasted, canned), chopped
7	flat anchovy fillets, drained
	Salt to taste
	Freshly ground pepper
¼	cup olive oil
3	small onions, peeled and thinly sliced
3	tablespoons chopped fresh cilantro
1	green sweet Italian pepper, seeded and cut in thin slices
4	tuna steaks (about ½ lb. each)
8	small stuffed olives for garnish

In a food processor or blender, add the garlic, tomatoes, bay leaves, pimento, anchovies, salt, and pepper and blend until smooth.

In a large skillet, heat the oil and sauté the onions, cilantro, and sweet pepper until onions are soft. Place the fish on top of the onion mixture and pour the sauce from the blender over the fish. Cover and cook over low heat for about 25 minutes or until the fish is done. Transfer the fish and sauce mixture to a serving platter and garnish with the stuffed olives.

Serve with hot crunchy bread.

Poultry / Aves

CHICKEN WITH GARLIC SAUCE
POLLO AL AJILLO

This is another favorite in Spanish restaurants. The combination of olive oil, fruity garlic, and Spanish paprika creates an aroma that will bring your neighbors knocking at your door. So make extra and invite your amigos. Maybe some relatives, too.

SERVES 4

    6   tablespoons olive oil
 2½   pounds chicken pieces
    8   cloves garlic, mashed
  ½   teaspoon paprika
  ¼   teaspoon crushed red pepper
  ½   cup (4 oz.) dry red wine
        Salt to taste
    6   orange slices for garnish

In a large skillet, heat the oil and sauté the chicken until golden brown. Remove to a warm platter.

In the same skillet, add the garlic, paprika, crushed red pepper, wine, and salt. Cook uncovered over medium heat for about 5 minutes. Return the chicken to the skillet, cover, and cook over low heat until the chicken is tender (about 20 minutes).

Transfer the chicken and the mixture to a serving platter and garnish with the orange slices.

Serve with Saffron Rice and a green vegetable.

DUCK WITH WINE SAUCE
PATO AL ESTÍLO DE SEVÍLLA

If the aroma from the herbs, spices, garlic, and onion doesn't wake up your appetite, the flambé finale will. The abundance of foods in Andalucía provides an endless variety of recipe ingredients. This classic duck recipe is simple to prepare and beautiful in its presentation.

SERVES 4

    1   whole duck (neck removed), about 4 pounds
        Vegetable shortening
  ¼   cup olive oil
    4   cloves garlic, mashed
    1   medium onion, chopped
  ½   teaspoon paprika
    3   tablespoons chopped flat parsley
    1   bay leaf

¼	teaspoon dried thyme
¼	cup (2 oz.) Licor 43
¼	cup (2 oz.) brandy
½	cup (4 oz.) dry white wine
½	cup chicken broth
12	baby carrots, whole
	Salt to taste
	Freshly ground pepper
3	tablespoons chopped parsley for garnish

Baste the duck with vegetable shortening and place it in a broiler pan. Bake in a 350°F preheated oven for about 1 ½ hours or until the duck is lightly golden. Remove and drain. Cut the duck into serving pieces and set aside on a warm platter.

In a large deep skillet, heat the oil and sauté the garlic, onion, paprika, parsley, bay leaf, and thyme until onion is soft. Add the duck pieces, the liqueur, and the brandy and flambé (be very careful) until flames subside. Add the wine, broth, carrots, salt, and pepper and mix well. Cover and cook over low heat for about 30 minutes or until the duck is tender. Discard bay leaf.

Remove duck and mixture to a serving platter and sprinkle with the parsley.

Serve with a baked potato or your favorite pasta.

TURKEY ANDALUCIAN STYLE
PAVO ANDALUZ

The turkey comes from Mexico, where it was found by a naturalist traveling with Columbus. It was called guajolote *by the American natives. The English believed Columbus had sailed to the East and so they named the big bird for a country called Turkey. The Spanish compared the turkey to a pheasant and called it* gallopavo. *You will call it* delicioso.

SERVES 10

1	12–14 pound turkey
10	orange slices for garnish

MARINADE
  6   cloves garlic, peeled
  2   tablespoons salt
  2   teaspoons freshly ground pepper
  3   tablespoons sherry wine vinegar
  1   teaspoon paprika
  ½   cup olive oil

STUFFING
  6   tablespoons olive oil
  1   medium onion, peeled and chopped
  4   cloves garlic, peeled and mashed
  ½   cup chopped serrano or prosciutto ham
  1   green bell pepper, seeded and chopped
  3   tablespoons chopped fresh cilantro
  2½ pounds ground lean pork
  ¼   cup (2 oz.) dry white wine
  ¼   cup chopped almonds
  ¼   cup raisins
  1   tablespoon capers
  ¼   cup chopped canned pimentos
  2   cups peeled and finely shredded green plantains
      Salt to taste
      Freshly ground pepper

BASTING MIXTURE
  ½   cup butter
  3   tablespoons honey
  ½   cup (4 oz.) dry sherry
  ½   cup orange juice
      Cheesecloth to cover turkey

In a food processor or blender, place all the ingredients for the marinade and blend until smooth. Rub the turkey inside and out with the marinade mixture and set aside in the refrigerator for about 3 hours or overnight.

For the stuffing, heat the oil in a large skillet and sauté the onion, garlic, ham, green pepper, and cilantro until onion is soft. Add the ground pork and wine and mix well. Cover and cook over medium heat for about 10 minutes or until meat is brown. Then add the almonds, raisins, capers, pimentos, plantains, salt, and pepper to taste and mix well. Cook, uncovered, for about 5 minutes, mixing occasionally. Remove from heat. Stuff the turkey with the mixture three-quarters full. Tie the legs together and fold the wings back. Secure the opening with metal skewers and set aside.

For the basting mixture, melt the butter in a small saucepan over low heat and add the honey, sherry, and orange juice and mix well. Remove, set aside, and let cool. Soak the cheesecloth in the melted butter mixture and cover the turkey. (Reserve the rest of the butter mixture for later use.) Place the turkey (breast side up) in a 325°F preheated oven, basting with the reserved butter mixture occasionally, for about 4 hours or until the turkey is done. (Remove the cloth for the last ½ hour to brown.) Transfer the turkey to a carving board and garnish with the orange slices.

Serve with all the trimmings you can imagine.

Meat / Carnes

OXTAIL STEW RONDA STYLE
RABO DE TORO A LA RONDA

This classic dish comes from the area of the bullfights. Ronda is the name of the little town where bullfighting originated in 1710 by Fernando Pedro Romero, an ordinary carpenter who became a Spanish hero. This hearty recipe of meats, wine, and sauce celebrates the robust, earthy spirit of Andalucía. No bull.

SERVES 4

4	pounds oxtail, cut into 2-inch pieces
½	teaspoon paprika
	Freshly ground pepper
3	tablespoons olive oil
4	cloves garlic

    1   medium onion
    ¼   teaspoon cumin
    ¼   cup chopped serrano or prosciutto ham
    ¼   cup chopped chorizo
    3   tablespoons chopped flat parsley
    3   tablespoons flour
    1   cup strong beef bouillon
    1   cup (8 oz.) dry white wine
    ¼   cup (2 oz.) sherry
         Salt to taste
    3   sprigs parsley for garnish

Sprinkle the oxtail pieces with paprika and pepper. Place the oxtails in a broiler pan and bake in a 350°F preheated oven for about 1 hour, turning once. Drain and remove to a warm platter.

In a large deep skillet, heat the oil and sauté the garlic, onion, cumin, ham, chorizo, and chopped parsley until onion is soft. Add the flour and mix well until smooth, then add the bouillon, white wine, sherry, and salt and mix well. Add the oxtail pieces and bring to a boil.

Cover and cook over low heat for about 1½ hours or until meat is tender. Remove the oxtail and the mixture to a serving platter and garnish with the parsley sprigs.

Serve over rice.

VEAL WITH HONEY SAUCE
TERNERA A LA MIÉL

I first tried this dish at the home of my friend from Andalucía, Clemente Barcena. I was so fond of the recipe I asked his mother for it and put it on the menu in my restaurant. It became a specialty of the house and provides a unique flavor, a tender texture, and a memorable experiencia.

                                                        SERVES 4

    1   large onion, peeled and chopped
    1   large green bell pepper, seeded and chopped
    ½   cup honey
    ½   cup (4 oz.) white wine
    1   cup (8 oz.) dry sherry
    ½   cup beef broth or water

½   teaspoon crumbled saffron
1   tablespoon paprika
1   tablespoon salt (or less)
6   tablespoons olive oil
2½ pounds boneless veal, cut into 1-inch cubes
6   orange slices for garnish

In a food processor or blender, mix all the ingredients (in a few steps, if necessary) except the olive oil, the veal, and the garnish. Blend until smooth.

Place the meat in a large bowl and pour the mixture over the meat; mix well and marinate overnight in the refrigerator. Drain the meat and reserve the marinade.

In a large deep skillet, heat the oil and sauté the meat, shaking the pan briskly, until meat is lightly browned.

Pour the marinade over the meat and bring to a boil. Cover and cook over low heat for about 45 minutes. Then uncover and continue cooking until the sauce is slightly thickened.

Remove the meat and sauce to a serving platter and garnish with the orange slices.

I recommend you serve this with a side dish of Mushrooms in Sherry Sauce and one of my rice recipes or your favorite pasta.

LAMB STEW, GRANADA STYLE
CORDERO A LA GRANÁDA

Lamb is one of the favorite meats in southern Spain. It teams well with spices, especially garlic. This dish reminds me of my grandmother's kitchen. Rústica y auténtica.

SERVES 4

2½ pounds boneless lamb, cut into 2-inch cubes
6   cloves garlic, chopped
1   tablespoon paprika
1   tablespoon dried oregano
3   bay leaves, crumbled
1   teaspoon crushed red pepper
¼   cup sherry wine vinegar
1½ cups (12 oz.) dry white wine

½   teaspoon salt (or less)
¼   cup olive oil
4   cups beef broth
    Salt to taste

In a food processor or blender, combine the garlic, paprika, oregano, bay leaves, crushed red pepper, vinegar, ½ cup of the wine, and ½ teaspoon salt. Blend until sauce is smooth.

Place the meat in a bowl and cover with the marinade. Mix well. Cover and place in refrigerator overnight.

In a large deep skillet, heat the oil and sauté the meat for about 3 minutes, shaking the pan often. Remove the meat to a warm platter. Add the remaining wine, beef broth, and the reserved marinade and bring to a boil. Add the meat, cover, and cook over low heat for about 1 ½ hours or until the meat is tender.

Transfer the meat to a serving platter. Continue cooking the sauce to desired consistency. Check for seasoning and pour sauce over the meat.

Serve with your favorite rice or pasta dish.

PORK IN GARLIC SAUCE
CERDO AL AJILLO

I can never stay away from garlic and olive oil. And this is one of those dishes that is close to my heart. Don't worry about too much garlic. It's never too much garlic.

SERVES 4

2½   pounds boneless pork, cut into 2-inch cubes
    Salt to taste
    Freshly ground pepper
8   cloves garlic, peeled
3   tablespoons chopped flat parsley
¼   cup chopped onion
2   cups (16 oz.) dry white wine
¼   cup olive oil
1½   cups beef broth
2   red bell peppers, seeded and coarsely chopped
½   teaspoon dried oregano, or 1 tablespoon of fresh chopped

¼   teaspoon dried thyme, or 1 teaspoon of fresh
        chopped
1   bay leaf
6   orange slices for garnish

Sprinkle the meat with salt and pepper and set aside.

In a food processor or blender, add the garlic, parsley, onion, and 1 cup of the wine. Blend until smooth. Reserve.

In a large skillet, heat the oil and sauté the meat (shaking the pan briskly) until meat is browned on all sides. Remove the meat to a warm platter.

In the same skillet, add the mixture from the blender, along with the broth, remaining wine, bell peppers, oregano, thyme, bay leaf, and salt and pepper to taste. Mix well and cook over medium heat for about 10 minutes.

Return the meat to the skillet and mix well with the sauce. Cover and cook at low heat for about 1 hour or until the meat is tender. Remove the meat to a serving platter and continue cooking the sauce until desired consistency. Check for seasoning. Discard bay leaf. Pour the sauce over the meat and garnish with the orange slices.

Serve this dish with a Vegetable Medley and one of my Spanish rice recipes.

Desserts / Postres

FIGS WITH CHOCOLATE AND WALNUTS
HIGOS CON CHOCOLATE

The sunny, hot summers and lush orchards of Andalucía produce figs of incredible sweetness and texture. In America figs like this are available in late summer and early fall. Combine them with melted chocolate and crunchy walnuts and you will create a dessert that is deliciously wicked. Your friends will love it.

SERVES 4

1   cup semisweet melting chocolate pieces
½   cup evaporated milk

¼   cup finely ground shelled walnuts
¼   cup (2 oz.) Licor 43
16   fresh figs, with stems

In a double boiler, combine the chocolate, milk, walnuts, and liqueur. Melt over low heat, stirring constantly, until sauce is smooth and thickened.

Dip each fig by the stem into the sauce and then into a bowl of ice water. Remove to a serving platter and repeat the process.

GLAZED ALMONDS
ALMENDRAS GARRAPIÑADAS

Nuts are one of Spain's finest crops, and this recipe is an Andalucían tradition. Make plenty because they won't last long.

SERVES 4

1½   teaspoons water
½   cup sugar
½   cup butter
1   teaspoon Licor 43
½   cup slivered almonds

In a small saucepan, combine the water, sugar, butter, and liqueur. Melt over low heat until the sugar caramelizes. Add the almonds and mix quickly with a fork. Working quickly, turn the caramelized almond mixture over a greased cookie sheet and spread with the fork. Let cool.

When cool, break into small pieces (about 2-inch squares).

HEAVENLY DESSERT
TOCINO DE CIELO

This recipe was created by nuns in 1611. The winemakers of southern Spain used egg whites to clarify their wine. By order of Philip III the yolks were given to nuns of the order of Clarisa. After many centuries in the convent kitchen, the recipe became part of the regional tradition and is considered one of the postres finos *of all of Spain.*

1 tablespoon water
7 tablespoons fine sugar
¼ cup water
1 cup fine sugar
1 tablespoon brandy
½ teaspoon cinnamon
   2″ peel of a lemon
6 egg yolks
2 whole eggs
   Whipped cream for garnish
   Fresh mint leaves for garnish

In a small pan, place 1 tablespoon water and 7 tablespoons sugar and mix well. Cook over low heat until sugar caramelizes. Coat the bottom and sides of 4 dessert molds with the caramelized sugar and set aside.

In the same pan, add ¼ cup water, 1 cup sugar, brandy, cinnamon, and lemon peel. Cook over medium heat until sauce reaches a fine consistency. Remove from the heat and discard the lemon peel.

In a medium bowl, add the 6 egg yolks and the 2 whole eggs and beat gently with a fork. Add the syrup to the eggs in a slow stream, mixing gently to prevent curdling.

Strain the mixture through a fine strainer into a pouring container.

Pour the mixture into the molds and place the molds inside a larger pan containing water to a depth of about 1 inch. Cover the pan with aluminum foil and tuck the corners around the pan.

Place the pan in a 350°F preheated oven for about 15 minutes or until mixture is dry. (Be very careful of steam when opening the foil.) Remove the molds from the pan and let cool at room temperature. Unmold by passing a knife around the edges. Flip each mold over a dessert plate, scooping as much syrup as possible. Garnish the top with 1 teaspoon whipped cream and a mint leaf.

The Old Archway at Trujillo

EXTREMADURA

Extremadura is the cradle of conquistadors. The westernmost region of Spain, it was thoroughly occupied and sacked by the Moorish invaders who vainly tried to bury all traces of Christian culture. The wars of reconquest, followed by the Napoleonic invasions, left Extremadura desolate and impoverished. Population shrank and the harshness of life increased. From these hard times came the bold, fearless adventurers who carried the Spanish flag beyond their shores and planted it all over the New World. Hernando Cortés, conqueror of Mexico and Central America; Francisco Pizarro, conqueror of Perú and the entire Inca civilization; Vasco de Balboa, who sailed the Pacific Ocean and discovered the coastline of western America: these are a few of the heroic names of Spanish history. Their expeditions were filled with the men of Extremadura—tough, nothing-to-lose mercenaries who followed the promise of wealth and adventure. Life in the New World, at any price offered more than a homeland racked for centuries by war and conquest.

Today, Extremadura exists quietly and beautifully under the dry Spanish sun. Roman bridges, theaters, aqueducts, and roads retain their magnificence as monuments to a great empire whose art and engineering stand tall after almost 2,000 years. Moorish castles overlook rolling hillsides and offer faded memories of unlimited luxury and pleasure. There are medieval monasteries built during the fervent period of Virgin worship. The city of Guadalupe was the sight of the unearthing of an early Christian idol, the Virgin of Guadalupe, which had been stolen and hidden in a "grave" by the Moorish invaders. Its resurrection instigated a pilgrimage period that brought passionate Spanish Catholics to Extremadura by the thousands to kiss the carved wooden face of the sacred statue. Religion and monasteries flourished. Monks became collectors of sacred art and religious objects. These treasures are displayed today in the restored monasteries that serve as hotels, called paradors. Many of the medieval castles and Arab palaces have also become paradors and offer the guest a journey into history.

Like the religion they served, the monks of Extremadura had a tremendous impact on the region. The monasteries became the center for pilgrims, religious artists, political intrigue—and culinary practice. During the Napoleonic invasion of the early 1800s, a monastery near Alcántara was sacked. Hand-scribed parchments were confiscated to wad up for rifle loading. One of the manuscripts saved was the record of recipes used in the monastery kitchens. It was taken back to France. *Consumado* became *consommé*; the secrets of truffles were revealed; and a Spanish country food became *pâté de foie gras*, synonymous with French royalty. These popular French dishes were created from these stolen Spanish recipes, a testimony to the high level of Spanish cuisine that has existed for centuries even in a remote place like Extremadura.

The kitchens of Extremadura produce many meals made with lamb or goat that's been roasted, stewed, fried, or baked. Game is plentiful, including pheasant, quail, and partridge. Pork is popular in the form of ham. Extremadura is the creative center for *jamón serrano*. This specially cured ham seasoned with paprika is a basic ingredient for many *tapas*, salads, and vegetable recipes. Thinly, thinly sliced and served with fresh yellow melon and crushed black pepper, *jamón serrano* is an exquisite appetizer.

Spicy, crushed red pepper is produced in the hot dry climate, and thousands of peppers are prepared for export. Table vegetables are simple and abundant. Cauliflower is a traditional favorite, but tomatoes, beans, potatoes, onions, peppers, and garlic are other staples. Extremadura cooking is based on very old traditions, carefully recorded by the monastery scribes and practiced in the same manner for centuries. Change is not the way of life in Extremadura, but its interesting and time-tested cuisine will bring a delicious change to your table.

THE WINES OF EXTREMADURA

The wines of Extremadura are limited and local. They do, however, possess the unusual characteristic of developing a yeast layer, much like the sherry wines of Jerez. This creates a wine with a distinct fragrance and an earthy taste.

Appetizers / Tapas

CHORIZOS AND OLIVES
ACEITUNAS CON CHORIZO

Chorizo is everywhere in Spain. It is a Spanish original, but it is a specialty of Extremadura. The combination of lean meats, paprika, and the mix of spices particular to each chorizo maker produces a robust taste that stimulates a demand for more. Add the sweet, almost succulent taste of imported, roasted pimentos and you've got an enormous variety of flavor in a small appetizer. The bittersweet olive is the final taste touch. Served with wine or sherry, this is one of the most interesting of all the tapas.

SERVES 4

3	tablespoons olive oil
4	chorizos, each cut into 4 pieces
2	cloves garlic, peeled
¼	cup (2 oz.) brandy
16	slices canned pimento about ½" wide
16	toothpicks
16	small stuffed olives

In a large skillet, heat the oil and sauté the chorizos and garlic until they start to color. Remove the chorizos, discard the garlic, and drain the fat. Return the chorizos to the skillet and add the brandy and flambé (be very careful) until the flames subside.

Remove the chorizos to a serving platter. Wrap each piece of chorizo with a slice of pimento and secure with a toothpick. Place one olive at the end of the toothpick and arrange on the serving platter.

BAR-B-Q PORK
CERDO A LA PARRILLA

Although the Moors didn't eat pork, the idea of marination and shish kabob cooking is definitely an Arab culinary tradition that took root and has become part of classic Spanish cooking. Marination soaks the meat so it remains juicy and tender even though it is cooked over an open flame without water or steam. So before you barbecue, marinate and put on your funny apron.

SERVES 4 – 6

1	pound pork, cut into 1-inch cubes
16	thin slices French bread, cut diagonally
2	tablespoons chopped fresh parsley for garnish

MARINADE

3	cloves garlic, peeled
1	tablespoon chopped onion
¼	teaspoon oregano
1	teaspoon paprika
1	teaspoon red wine vinegar
¼	teaspoon cayenne pepper
2	tablespoons red wine
½	teaspoon salt (or less)
¼	teaspoon freshly ground pepper
5	tablespoons olive oil

In a food processor or blender, mix all the marinade ingredients and blend until smooth.

Place the meat in a medium bowl and pour the marinade over it. Mix well to cover the meat. Cover the bowl and refrigerate overnight. Remove the meat from the marinade (reserve the marinade) and place 4 to 5 meat cubes on a small skewer. Repeat the process until all cubes have been skewered.

Place the skewers under a broiler or on top of a barbecue grill and baste with the marinade until meat is done.

Remove the meat and place it on top of the slices of bread and remove the skewers. Sprinkle the meat cubes with the chopped parsley and serve.

Vegetables / Legumbres

GREEN BEANS AND POTATOES
PATATAS Y JUDIAS VERDES

This is a traditional dish that began with the discovery of the New World. The American natives of Peru grew a wide variety of tubers called papus, *while the Haitian islanders grew a yam called* batata. *So between the two New World discoveries the Spanish created* patata, *or potato. Sweet green beans grew everywhere in Spain, and when you eat them in this dish with small, thin-skinned new potatoes, cilantro, white wine, and cheese, you will discover a whole new dimension to vegetables.*

SERVES 4

3	tablespoons olive oil
3	tablespoons butter (or less)
2	cups white potatoes, peeled and diced
3	cloves garlic, mashed
½	cup chopped onion
3	tablespoons chopped fresh cilantro
¼	cup (2 oz.) dry white wine
½	pound green beans, tips removed, cut into 1-inch pieces
	Salt to taste
2	tablespoons grated Parmesan cheese for garnish (optional)

In a large skillet, heat the oil and butter and sauté the potatoes over medium heat for about 10 minutes or until potatoes are barely tender. Add the garlic, onion, and cilantro and mix well for about 3 minutes. Add the wine, beans, and salt to taste and mix well. Cover and cook over low heat for about 20 minutes or until the beans are tender.

Remove the beans and potato mixture to a serving platter and sprinkle with the cheese.

POTATOES AND GREENS
PATATAS Y ACELGAS

Don't give up on greens because your family says they don't like them. Make this recipe. The sweet, tender new potatoes and the mix of leafy green flavors sautéed with spices and topped with beaten eggs is a dish they will love. It is also a nutritional powerhouse. But don't tell your family it's good for them.

SERVES 4

 5 tablespoons olive oil
16 small new potatoes, scrubbed and blanched
 3 cloves garlic, mashed
 1 cup chopped onion
 3 tablespoons chopped fresh cilantro
½ teaspoon paprika
½ cup chicken broth
   Salt to taste
   Freshly ground pepper
 1 pound cleaned mixed greens (collards, turnip tops,
      beet tops, escarole, etc.), stems removed, coarsely
      chopped
 2 beaten eggs or egg substitute equivalent
 3 orange slices for garnish

In a large deep skillet, heat the oil and sauté the potatoes until light golden. Add the garlic, onion, cilantro, paprika, broth, and salt and pepper to taste. Mix well and bring to a boil. Add the greens and mix well. Cover and cook over low heat about 5–8 minutes until the greens are tender. Pour the eggs over the mixture; cover and continue cooking until eggs are firm and not runny.

Remove the mixture to a serving platter and garnish with the orange slices.

Soups / Sopas

WHITE GAZPACHO
GAZPACHO EXTREMEÑO

It's a hot summer day. You don't feel like cooking, but you're hungry. You don't feel like going to the store but all you have is some odds and ends in the cupboard and the refrigerator. Perfect. Make this recipe. Gazpacho, from the Latin caspa, *means "bits and pieces." You can even add a touch of your own or change some of mine. No cooking. No fuss. Just the blender, your imagination, and this recipe. By the way, it was a favorite of Eugenia de Montigo, wife of Napoleon III. She didn't like to cook on a hot day, either.*

SERVES 4

2	cloves garlic, peeled
1	tablespoon chopped onion
1	small cucumber, peeled and chopped
¼	teaspoon dried thyme
¼	teaspoon dried crushed red pepper
½	teaspoon dried tarragon
3	tablespoons red wine vinegar
¼	teaspoon sugar (or less)
1	medium green bell pepper, seeded and chopped
1	bay leaf, crumbled
1	egg (optional) or egg substitute equivalent
1	teaspoon chopped flat parsley
1	teaspoon salt (or less)
¼	teaspoon freshly ground pepper
4	slices bread, crust removed
6	tablespoons olive oil
3	cups cold water
	Seasoned croutons for garnish

In a food processor or blender, mix all the ingredients (in a few steps if necessary) except the garnish and blend well until smooth. Pour the mixture into a large bowl and chill.

To serve, pour the mixture into individual soup bowls and garnish with the croutons.

CONSOMMÉ EXTREMADURA STYLE
CONSUMADO A LA EXTREMEÑA

*When the Napoleonic armies ransacked the monasteries of Extremadura, they confiscated the handwritten recipes of the monastery kitchens. Among many classic Spanish recipes that had been carefully guarded from as early as the Roman conquest was the recipe for con-*sumado. *When this recipe reappeared on the royal tables of France it was called consommé. That name is used everywhere in the Western world today . . . except Spain, of course, which knows the real story. Now you do, too.*

SERVES 4−6

½	pound beef bones
1	pound lean beef, cut into chunks
7	cups cold water
1	leek, washed and sliced
1	stalk celery with leaves, cut in half
1	medium onion, peeled, stuck with 2 cloves
½	tablespoon salt (or less)
1	carrot, scrubbed and cut into chunks
4	peppercorns
1	sprig flat parsley
¼	teaspoon thyme
1	clove garlic, peeled
1	small bay leaf
2	egg whites, beaten
1	finely chopped tomato for garnish

In a large casserole (6 quarts), combine the bones, beef, and water and bring to a boil. Cover and cook over low heat for about 1 hour, skimming off the fat with a skimmer. Add the rest of the ingredients except the egg whites and the tomato and bring to a boil. Cover and cook over low heat for about 4 hours. Strain the broth through a double thickness of cheesecloth and skim off the fat. Reserve the meat for later use and discard the vegetables and bones. Return the broth to the casserole. Add the egg whites and bring to a boil.

Strain the broth through a double thickness of cheesecloth and pour the broth into individual soup bowls. Garnish with chopped tomato and serve.

Eggs / Platos de Huevos

VEGETABLES WITH HAM AND EGGS
HUEVOS ESTILO EXTREMEÑA

What a brunch! Toast some rolls. Chill some orange juice. This is a hearty, robust meal that is filled with fresh ingredients, plenty of protein, and a sparkle of wine and spices. It is a traditional Extremadurian favorite that's been part of classic Spanish cuisine for almost 500 years. So you know they know what they're doing.

SERVES 4

¼	cup olive oil
1	pound small new potatoes, blanched
1	large onion, peeled and chopped
2	cloves garlic, peeled and mashed
1	tablespoon chopped fresh cilantro
½	cup chopped smoked ham
1	cup canned crushed tomatoes
¼	cup (2 oz.) dry white wine
2	large carrots, peeled and thinly sliced
	Salt to taste
	Freshly ground pepper
4	large eggs
2	tablespoons chopped parsley for garnish

In a large skillet, heat the oil and sauté the potatoes, shaking the pan briskly, until potatoes are light golden. Add the onion, garlic, cilantro, and ham; mix well and cook until the onion is soft. Add the tomatoes, wine, carrots, and salt and pepper to taste. Bring to a boil, cover, and cook over low heat for about 15 minutes and mix well.

Crack the eggs and arrange them separately on top of the tomato mixture. Cover and continue cooking over low heat until the whites of the eggs are done.

Remove each egg with some of the mixture and place on individual serving plates. Sprinkle with chopped parsley.

Poultry / Aves

PHEASANT IN MADEIRA WINE
FAISAN DE ALCANTARA

In long-ago times, pheasant was the food of the farmers and their families. Wild game was abundant and pheasants feeding on the fallen grains in the fields were easy game. Foreign conquest, social evolution, and industrial revolution made the pheasant a luxury food for the nobility. This classic recipe was among the rare hand-scribed recipes looted from the Benedictine monasteries and taken to France. It was during this time that pheasant moved up the social ladder from the farmyard to the golden platters of Versailles, where it has remained. In addition to the pheasant itself, many classic recipes add the exotic flavor of truffles, which heightens the experience immensely, even though the cost may be extravagant. Nevertheless, its history and exquisite taste secure its position as one of the world's finest foods. I raise my glass to the people of history who created this masterpiece in Extremadura.

SERVES 4

2   young pheasants, 2–3 pounds each, fresh or frozen
    Salt to taste
    Freshly ground pepper
2   small onions, peeled, with 2 cloves stuck in each
2   bay leaves
2   garlic cloves, peeled
4   orange slices
    Vegetable shortening
1   stick butter
1   cup (8 oz.) Madeira wine or dry sherry

2   ounces truffles or morels, cut into slices
     Cheesecloth
1   bunch parsley sprigs for garnish

Sprinkle the birds with salt and pepper inside and out. Place in each cavity one onion, one bay leaf, one garlic clove, and two orange slices. Tie the legs of the birds with a string and fold the wings backwards.

Rub the birds with the shortening and place them, breast side up, in a baking pan with a rack.

In a small saucepan, melt the butter with the wine. Let cool. Place the truffles in a food processor or blender. With the motor running, add the butter and wine mixture in a slow stream. Remove the blender mixture to a bowl and soak the cheesecloth with it. Cover the birds with the cheesecloth and place them in a 350°F preheated oven, basting with the reserved mixture occasionally for about 2 hours or until the birds are done.

Remove the cheesecloth and untie the legs. Transfer the birds to a serving platter and garnish with the parsley sprigs.

Serve with brandied poached fruits and tiny asparagus tips.

Meat / Carnes

LAMB WITH PAPRIKA AND SHERRY
COCHIFRITO DE CORDERO

Lamb cochifrito *is one of the oldest and most typical dishes of the region of Extremadura. The many flocks of sheep and family livestock provide a constant supply of this favorite meat. The nice thing about this recipe is its stove-top cooking and simple preparation. The covered pan and low flame make the meat tender and full of the flavor of the wine and spices. It is a basic, classic recipe, but its wonderful flavor and simple cooking make it* muy popular *today.*

SERVES 4

2   pounds boneless lamb, cut into chunks
     Salt to taste
     Freshly ground pepper

    1   tablespoon paprika
    ¼   cup olive oil
    ½   cup chopped onion
    4   cloves garlic, peeled and mashed
    ½   cup (4 oz.) dry sherry wine
    1   bay leaf
    3   orange slices for garnish
    3   sprigs parsley for garnish

Sprinkle the meat with salt, pepper, and paprika. Rub well and set aside for about 30 minutes.

In a large skillet, heat the oil and sauté the meat until brown. Remove to a warm platter and set aside. In the same skillet, sauté the onion and garlic until onion is soft. Add the wine, bay leaf, and reserved meat. Check for seasoning. Mix well, cover, and cook over low heat until the meat is tender.

Remove the meat and mixture to a serving platter. Discard the bay leaf. Garnish with the orange slices and parsley sprigs.

Serve with baby carrots and white rice.

VEAL, CHORIZO, AND PEPPERS
TERNERA ESTILO EXTREMEÑA

The Spanish dramatist Lope de Vega said, "Life is but an empty sham, without a slice of Spanish ham." So to keep our lives full we will make this dish with serrano ham. A classic Spanish creation, serrano is a small Spanish ham hung to dry and cured with paprika and olive oil. Serrano is best served cut very, very thin and served with fresh melon. It is less salty than most dried ham and is available in some specialty stores and Spanish supermarkets. In this recipe it adds a special taste, and its gentle flavor, along with the assertive chorizo, sweet green peppers, brandy, and sherry, adds the final touch to this festival de sabores.

SERVES 4

    2   pounds thinly sliced veal cutlets
         Salt to taste
         Freshly ground pepper
         Flour for dusting
    2   tablespoons olive oil
    2   tablespoons butter

2   cloves garlic, mashed
1   small onion, thinly sliced
¼   cup chopped chorizo
¼   cup chopped serrano or prosciutto ham
1   large green bell pepper, seeded and chopped
¼   cup chicken or beef broth
¼   cup (2 oz.) dry sherry
1   tablespoon brandy
½   cup canned crushed tomatoes
1   bay leaf, whole
3   orange slices for garnish
2   sprigs parsley for garnish

Sprinkle the cutlets with salt and pepper and dust with flour.

In a large skillet, heat the oil and butter and sauté the cutlets on both sides until golden. Set aside.

In the same skillet, combine the garlic, onion, chorizo, ham, and green peppers. Sauté for about 4 minutes or until the onions are soft. Add the broth, sherry, brandy, tomatoes, bay leaf, salt, and pepper. Mix well and cook for about 5 minutes more.

Return the cutlets to the skillet and mix well with the sauce. Cover and cook over low heat for about 15 minutes or until the cutlets are tender.

Remove the cutlets and mixture to a serving platter. Discard the bay leaf. Garnish with the orange slices and parsley.

Serve with Saffron Rice.

SAUSAGES WITH APPLES AND BRANDY
SALCHICHAS A LA EXTREMEÑA

This recipe was originally created with fresh meat sausage. Since fresh Spanish sausage is not easily found, use sweet Italian sausage. This dish is served at the beautiful Parador Nacional de Plata, an enormous old convent converted to hotel, restaurant, bar, and tourist attraction. Its presentation of this dish is beautiful, classic, and muy delicioso. *Eating this dish in such an environment steeped in history wafts you back to another time filled with conquistadors and adventure. Más chorizo and brandy,* por favor.

SERVES 4

2	tablespoons olive oil
1½	pounds sweet Italian sausages
5	tart medium apples, cored and cut into thin slices
¼	cup brown sugar
¼	cup (2 oz.) brandy
1	stick cinnamon

In a large skillet, heat the oil and sauté the sausages until light golden. Drain and remove the sausages to a baking pan. Arrange the apples around the sausages. Sprinkle the sugar, brandy, and cinnamon over the apples.

Cover the pan with aluminum foil and bake in a 375°F preheated oven for about 15 minutes or until the apples are tender.

Remove the sausages to a serving plate and cut into serving-size pieces. Mix the apples with the sauce and pour over the sausages.

Serve with Cauliflower Muleteer Style.

LAMB STEW WITH RED PEPPERS
CORDERO A LA EXTREMEÑA

There are two things you can surely count on in Extremadura: great, sweet red peppers and tender, succulent lamb. The boneless lamb in this recipe is cut into strips. When the dish is finished cooking it can be served with white rice or stuffed into fresh French bread for a meal in a sandwich. Maybe not classic, but a muy bueno *lunch.*

SERVES 4

¼	cup olive oil
1½	pounds boneless lamb, cut into strips
5	cloves garlic, mashed
1	large onion, peeled and chopped
¼	teaspoon crushed red pepper
1	tablespoon paprika
2	tablespoons chopped fresh cilantro
½	cup (4 oz.) dry sherry
½	cup beef broth
1	bay leaf
2	large red bell peppers, seeded and chopped
½	teaspoon salt (or less)

Freshly ground pepper
6   orange slices for garnish

In a large deep skillet, heat the oil and sauté the meat until it starts to color. Remove and set aside. In the same skillet sauté the garlic, onion, crushed red pepper, paprika, and cilantro until onion is soft. Add the sherry, broth, bay leaf, red bell pepper, and salt and pepper to taste. Mix well and bring to a boil. Cover and cook over low heat for about 30 minutes. Uncover, add the meat, and continue cooking for about 10 minutes more, or until the sauce starts to thicken and the meat is tender.

Discard bay leaf. Remove the meat and mixture to a serving platter and garnish with the orange slices.

Desserts / Postres

FRIED BREAD WITH BRANDY AND HONEY
FRITURAS DE MIEL

This classic Spanish dessert also makes a wonderful sweet Sunday morning breakfast. Either way, it loves hot coffee and fruit as companions. Call it postre *or call it* comida dulce.

SERVES 4

4   large eggs, slightly beaten, or egg substitute equivalent
½   cup orange-blossom honey
¼   cup (2 oz.) brandy
½   cup hot water
8   slices country-style bread
3   tablespoons olive oil
3   tablespoons butter (or less)
     Confectioner's sugar for dusting

In a medium bowl mix the eggs, honey, brandy, and water and blend until smooth. Transfer the mixture to a flat bowl and dip the bread to coat well.

In a large skillet, heat the oil and butter and fry the bread slices until light golden on both sides. Remove to a serving platter and sprinkle with the sugar.

Windmills at La Mancha

NEW CASTILE

New Castile is shepherds and windmills. Surrounded by mountains, it is the great flat treeless heart of Spain. It is a region that lies naked in the relentless summer sun and shivers throughout the bitter winters. New Castile is home to a hardy, frugal people who are descendants of a noble aristocracy that somehow lost its way and its fortune, but never its pride.

The land is visually simple and primal yet yields an enormous amount of wheat, grapes, game, and one of the world's most expensive crops: saffron. In late October, just after the grape harvest, the rolling, endless plains are painted purple with the blossoms of the crocus. It is a time for rejoicing and celebration. Everyone in every village, from the oldest *viejo* to the little children, becomes part of the process of creating the golden spice.

Saffron arrived in Spain with the Arabs who traded for it in their homeland from the caravans of the Orient. Called *za'faran* (or yellow) in Arabic, it is the most precious of the world's spices. Hundreds of thousands, even millions, of saffron flowers are carefully picked each morning and gently carried to great tables where the women and children peel each flower to expose the three red pistils in the heart of the blossom. These pistils are separated from the stamens and dried in the evening of the same day they are picked. Ten thousand flowers yield only 2 to 3 ounces of saffron, so little product for such labor. At five dollars or more a gram, this indispensable spice of Spain is treated like gold and its export is carefully monitored to maintain its quality and price.

Across the heart of New Castile lie the great plains of La Mancha. La Mancha comes from the Arab word Al Mancha, which means "flatlands." Windmills create the landscape and in the pink mists where the ocher earth meets the cerulean sky, the phantom image of Don

Quixote is a reflection of the forlorn noblemen, lost with their fortunes in times past, yet part of Castile today. The history of this region presents itself anew each day in a culture that never forgets its beginnings. Nowhere is the Castilian culture more evident than in its cuisine.

The region supports horizon-to-horizon fields of wheat which is milled then baked in centuries-old brick ovens to produce a round, crusty golden loaf with a pure white inside. It is easily the finest bread in Spain, if not all of Europe. These same "bakery" ovens are used to roast the very young lambs which are the special feast foods of the Castilian people. Shepherds roam the hills and the scrabby pastures tending their gentle flocks in a peaceful, loving way that stops time in a place long, long ago.

And where there is not wheat or saffron flowers or pasture, there are vineyards. The region of Castile produces more wine than any other in Spain. Most of it is for everyday consumption for it is not pressed or stored for vintage. It is a people's wine and is enjoyed where it is grown and pressed. If the huge, ancient, strange teardrop-shaped clay storage pots are not empty for the new pressing, the old wine is spilled to make room for the new. It is a culture that cannot separate itself from its earth; a testimony, perhaps, to the difficult terrain and to times when there was barely enough sustenance for the people.

Far from the sea, lacking in fertile soil, and locked in by mountains, Castile creates its cuisine from meat, game, potatoes, beans, legumes, eggs, cheese, and bread. Stews and soups are hearty and lusty. The famous *cocido castellano* is a rich, thick stew made with beef, chicken, bacon, and sausage with chick-peas, potatoes, and any other available vegetable. The soup is drained off and served as broth followed by a hearty platter of meats and vegetables. Chorizo, the small, hard, savory pork sausage heavily scented with garlic and paprika, is everywhere. Hunters' guns crack across the plains and a lone figure comes home with gun in hand and a shoulder bag full of hare, partridge, and quail.

Sheep's milk makes a cheese called Manchego, a variety found throughout Spain. Here in Castile, Manchego ranges from a tender, fresh snow-white delight to a dry, dark yellow, hard specimen with a strong sheep taste.

Throughout Old Castile all the foods are locally produced, except in the international capital city of Madrid and, to some extent, Toledo. In these cities, restaurants bring in food from all over Spain and are as sophisticated as any in the world. But the true spirit of Castilian cuisine is found in the old brick bread ovens, the suckling pig roasting pits, and the small white bag on the shepherd's hip in which he carries his lunch of bread, cheese, chorizo, and wine that he enjoys as he sits on a grassy hillside near his quiet flock.

THE WINES OF NEW CASTILE

Traditionally the vineyards of New Castile produced wines that were consumed locally. New technology and modern bottling facilities are making these hearty, delicious wines available outside of the region and beyond Spain. The last fifty years have seen some of the classic cooperative wineries replace the traditional clay *tinajas* with expoxy-lined concrete vats and stainless steel tanks. The age of modern vinification has come to Castile and we are all the beneficiaries.

From Valdepeñas in southern Castile comes a wine called "the red blood from the valley of the stones." Early transplants of the red Cencibel grape are mixed with large amounts of the white Arién. The Arién is a thick-skinned grape that resists the summer heat and produces a fresh, fruity taste. The blend of the Cencibel and Arién grapes creates a light red wine that has become popular in the bistros and tapas clubs of Madrid.

The plains of La Mancha produce an abundance of unblended wine from the Arién grape. Originally it was an earthy, heavy wine with above-average alcohol content, but new fermentation processes and earlier picking have created a lighter, more refreshing wine as well as some varieties with a definite fruity flavor. Several new cooperatives are producing blends of the wines of the region, and their whites, reds, and rosés have become quite popular in the United States.

East of La Mancha the small region of Almansa makes some outstanding red wines from the Monastrel and Garnacha grapes. Mostly sold for blending, the wines of the area are nevertheless excellent and fruity and have received several awards over the past several years.

In the province of Toledo in the area of Méntrida, the red Garnacha grape is grown. It produces a robust red wine with a high alcohol content. The wines are drunk young since they do not age well, but they have become part of the outstanding local wine lists and are very much in vogue throughout Toledo and Madrid.

Appetizers / Tapas

SNAILS IN PAPRIKA SAUCE
CARACOLES PICANTITOS

Snails, or caracoles, *became part of the world cuisine during Roman times. They were so popular with the Romans that entire fields of lettuce served as feeding beds for the succulent little mollusks. I have added my own touch of crushed red pepper to the taste of this classic recipe.*

SERVES 4

2	tablespoons olive oil
3	cloves garlic, mashed
1	cup chopped onion
½	cup chopped chorizo
1½	tablespoons paprika
½	teaspoon crushed red pepper
1	cup canned crushed tomatoes
1	cup (8 oz.) dry white wine
3	tablespoons chopped fresh cilantro
	Salt to taste
	Freshly ground pepper
20	canned snails in their shells, rinsed
4	lemon slices for garnish

In a large skillet, heat the oil and sauté the garlic, onion, chorizo, paprika, and the crushed red pepper for about 3 minutes or until the onion is soft.

Add the tomatoes, wine, cilantro, salt, pepper, and snails. Mix well to coat. Cover and cook over medium-low heat for about 20 minutes. Mix well.

Transfer the snails to a serving platter and continue cooking the sauce, uncovered, for about 2 more minutes. Mix well and pour the sauce over the snails.

Garnish with the lemon slices and serve hot with slices of crusty garlic bread.

STUFFED MUSSELS WITH HAM
MEJILLONES A LA MADRID

I first heard of this dish from my mother when she returned from a trip to Madrid in 1975. She was very excited as she tried to explain the recipe to me. Almost immediately I went into the kitchen, rolled up my sleeves, and came up with this winner. I hope it's a winner for you, too.

SERVES 4

¼	cup (2 oz.) dry white wine
½	cup clam broth
16	large mussels in their shells, well scrubbed and beards removed
2	cloves garlic, peeled
¼	cup chopped onion
1	tablespoon tomato sauce
¼	cup bread crumbs
1½	tablespoons chopped fresh cilantro
2	tablespoons chopped serrano or prosciutto ham
½	teaspoon salt
	Freshly ground pepper
3	tablespoons olive oil
1	teaspoon Licor 43
3	tablespoons chopped fresh parsley for garnish

In a large saucepan, add the wine, broth, and mussels and bring to a boil. Cover and simmer over low heat. As they open, remove the mussels to a warm platter. Reserve ½ cup of the liquid and set aside. Remove the meat from the mussels and reserve half of the shells.

In a food processor or blender, add the meat from the mussels, garlic, onion, tomato sauce, bread crumbs, cilantro, ham, salt, pepper, olive oil, and the liqueur. Blend until smooth.

Fill each shell with the mixture and place them in an oiled or buttered baking pan facing up. Bake in a 350°F preheated oven for about 10 minutes or until they plump. Then place them under a broiler until golden.

Transfer the mussels to a serving platter and sprinkle with the chopped parsley.

Salads / Ensaladas

CODFISH SALAD
ENSALADA DE BACALAO

Don't know what to do with dried cod? I do. Just follow my recipe and all the secrets of this special fish will become clear to you. And you'll create a salad that's the lambada *of* ensalada.

SERVES 4

- ¾ pound dried codfish fillets
- 6 cups water
- 1 large Spanish onion, peeled and sliced
- 2 medium tomatoes, sliced
- 8 small stuffed olives
- 1 green bell pepper, seeded and sliced

DRESSING
- 2 cloves garlic, peeled
- ½ cup virgin olive oil
- 3 tablespoons red wine vinegar
-    Salt to taste
- ¼ teaspoon freshly ground pepper

Place the codfish in a bowl of water and soak overnight, changing the water about 2 times. Drain well. In a large saucepan, bring 6 cups water to a boil. Place the codfish in the boiling water for 15 minutes. Drain and dry well. Shred the fish with a fork, place it in a serving bowl, and garnish with the onion, tomato, olives, and bell peppers. Set aside.

In a food processor or blender, mix all the ingredients for the dressing and blend until smooth. Pour the dressing over the salad, mix well, and serve chilled.

Vegetables / Legumbres

VEGETABLE MEDLEY
PISTO A LA MANCHA

La Mancha comes from the Arabic word meaning flatlands, but this La Mancha dish is anything but flat. It is a classic vegetable meal that pays honor to its history. ¡Viva Don Quixote!

SERVES 4

3	tablespoons olive oil
2	cloves garlic, mashed
1	large onion, peeled and chopped
2	chopped chorizos
2	tablespoons chopped flat parsley
1	medium potato, cut into ¼-inch rounds
2	medium zucchini, cut into ¼-inch rounds
1	medium yellow squash, cut into ¼-inch rounds
1	large tomato, chopped
1	green bell pepper, seeded and coarsely chopped
1	red bell pepper, seeded and coarsely chopped
¾	cup chicken broth
	Salt to taste
2	sprigs parsley for garnish

In a large deep skillet, heat the oil and sauté the garlic, onion, chorizos, and parsley until onion is soft. Add the potato, zucchini, yellow squash, tomato, bell peppers, broth, and salt. Mix well. Cover and cook over low heat for about 20 minutes or until the vegetables are soft.

Transfer the mixture to a serving bowl and garnish with the sprigs of parsley.

ASPARAGUS IN SAFFRON SAUCE
ESPARRAGOS AL AZAFRAN

This vegetable dish should be made with fresh asparagus. It comes from the land of saffron, which adds a golden color and exciting flavor to this dish. The combination of spices reflects years of Arab influence on Spanish cuisine.

SERVES 4

16   asparagus tips, blanched
 4   sprigs parsley for garnish

DRESSING
 1   clove garlic, peeled
 1   egg yolk or 2 slices of bread, crust removed
¼   teaspoon cumin
     Salt to taste
⅛   teaspoon crumbled saffron
¼   cup boiling water
¾   cup olive oil (or less)

Arrange the asparagus on a serving platter and set aside.

In a food processor or blender, mix the dressing ingredients except the olive oil and blend until smooth. With the motor running, pour the olive oil in a thin stream until sauce is thick.

Pour the dressing over the asparagus and garnish with the parsley sprigs.

POTATOES IN PAPRIKA SAUCE
PATATAS A LA ALBACETE

This recipe from the area of Albacete is one of my favorite dishes. Potatoes are usually bland, so if you like a little spice in your life, use hot paprika or add a dash of cayenne. Aii, aii, aii . . . Patatas al Diablo.

SERVES 4

½   cup olive oil
 3   medium baking potatoes, peeled and cut into thin
        slices
¼   cup chopped onion

3   cloves garlic, peeled
1   teaspoon paprika
1   bay leaf
1   tablespoon flour
1   cup clear chicken broth
    Salt to taste
2   tablespoons chopped parsley for garnish
3   orange slices for garnish

In a large skillet, heat the oil and sauté the potatoes, a few at a time. As they turn lightly golden on both sides, remove to the side of the skillet as you add more slices. Rotate uncooked slices underneath cooked potatoes. When all potatoes are cooked, add the onion and cook over medium heat for about 3 minutes or until onions are soft.

Meanwhile, in a food processor or blender combine the garlic, paprika, bay leaf, flour, broth, and salt to taste. Blend until smooth. Pour the mixture over the potatoes and mix well.

Cover and cook over low heat until the sauce has thickened and the potatoes are soft.

Transfer the potatoes and mixture to a serving platter and garnish with the chopped parsley and orange slices.

Serve with your favorite fish.

Soups / Sopas

GARLIC EGG SOUP CASTILIAN STYLE
SOPA CASTELLANA

My grandmother was an expert at making this soup. For years I wondered what was that special spice she used. One day I watched carefully and read the label on the jar after she took her two or three pinches. It was cumin. Now I share the secret with you. Okay, Grandma?

SERVES 4

¼   cup olive oil
4   thin slices French bread

1   teaspoon granulated garlic
4   cloves garlic, peeled and sliced
5   cups beef broth
1   tablespoon paprika
½   teaspoon crumbled saffron
½   teaspoon cumin
    Salt to taste
    Freshly ground pepper
4   large whole eggs or egg substitute equivalent
1   teaspoon chopped parsley for garnish

In a large deep skillet, heat 2 tablespoons of the oil and fry the bread until golden on both sides. Sprinkle with the granulated garlic on both sides and set aside.

In the same skillet, heat the remaining oil and sauté the sliced garlic until lightly golden. Add the broth, paprika, saffron, cumin, salt, and pepper and mix well. Cook, uncovered, over medium heat for about 5 minutes. Transfer the soup to 4 individual ovenproof crocks or bowls.

Crack one egg into each bowl. Place one slice of the fried toast on top of each bowl and place them in a 425°F preheated oven for about 3 minutes or until the whites of the eggs are set.

Remove from the oven and sprinkle the toast with the chopped parsley.

MADRID STEW
COCIDO MADRILEÑO

This cocido was introduced into Spain more than 700 years ago by the Spanish Sephardic Jews. Even though many changes have been made to this authentic classic stew over the years, it is still one of a kind. You could contribute to the variations, too.

If you have a pressure cooker, you can save a lot of time during the first part of the preparation.

SERVES 6−8

1   cup (8 oz.) red wine
13 cups water
2   tablespoons olive oil

1   pound chicken pieces, skinned
1   pound stewing beef, cut into chunks
1   pound boneless pork loin, cut into chunks
3   chorizos, cut into pieces
1   large onion, peeled and coarsely chopped
5   cloves garlic, peeled and mashed
4   medium potatoes, peeled and cut into halves
2   medium parsnips, cut into halves
½   teaspoon freshly ground pepper
     Salt to taste
½   pound thin spaghetti
2½   cups shredded cabbage
4   cups canned or fresh cooked chick-peas, drained
¼   cup chopped flat parsley

MEATBALLS
1½   pounds lean ground beef
1   egg
¼   cup bread crumbs
¼   teaspoon salt
¼   teaspoon paprika

In a large casserole (6 quarts), combine all the ingredients except the spaghetti, cabbage, chick-peas, parsley, and meatballs. Bring to a boil. Cover and cook over low heat for about 3 hours, occasionally removing the foam with a skimmer.

In a bowl, thoroughly mix all the ingredients for the meatballs. Make 4 to 6 meatballs of about 2-inch diameter. Set aside.

Add the spaghetti, cabbage, peas, parsley, and the meatballs to the stew. Continue cooking, covered, for about 45 minutes more. Pour the stew into individual soup bowls and garnish with the chopped parsley.

Serve with toasted French bread.

Rice / Arrozes

SAFFRON RICE
ARROZ CON AZAFRÁN

Saffron is the world's most expensive spice, and the finest in the world is produced in La Mancha. It comes from the crocus plant and takes 50,000 flowers to make one pound of spice. The Arab conquerors introduced the spice and the rice it goes with. These Moorish conquerors rebuilt the Roman irrigation system and created the wet rice lands. This recipe is a classic combination of these two most important Arab contributions to classic Spanish cooking. It goes with almost any Spanish dish and is muy sabrosa.

SERVES 4

3	tablespoons olive oil
1	small onion, peeled and chopped
3	cloves garlic, mashed
3	cups chicken broth
½	teaspoon crumbled saffron
1½	cups uncooked rice
	Salt to taste

Heat the oil in a large casserole and sauté the onion and garlic until onion is soft. Add the chicken broth and saffron and bring to a boil. Stir in the rice and salt to taste. Cook over medium-high heat uncovered for about 10 minutes or until rice is semi-dry but some liquid remains. Cover and cook over low heat for about 20 minutes. Turn rice over with a fork from bottom to top, cover, and cook for 10 more minutes.

Serve alongside a seafood or meat dish, and don't forget to invite your amigos.

Egg Dishes / Tortillas

SPANISH OMELET
TORTILLA ESPAÑOLA

It is said that more than two hundred years ago a Spanish king was hunting with his men in the countryside. At the end of the day they were lost and hungry. Searching for a place to eat, they came across a farmer's house. "I beg you, give us something to eat," entreated the king. The farmer picked up a few eggs and quickly sautéed them in a large skillet. The king exclaimed, "¡Que hombre mas lijero!" ("What a fast man!"). The person who wrote this story was a Frenchman. Since in French the word for man is homme *and for fast is* lette, *this is the story of the omelet, believe it or not.*

SERVES 4

    Oil for frying potatoes
2   large baking potatoes, peeled and cut into thin slices
6   tablespoons olive oil
4   large eggs or egg substitute equivalent
2   tablespoons water
    Salt to taste
    Freshly ground pepper
1   medium onion, coarsely chopped
1   tablespoon chopped parsley for garnish

Heat the oil in a large skillet and add the potato slices a few at a time. Cook over medium heat until they are soft.

Meanwhile, in a large bowl beat the eggs with 2 tablespoons water until they are slightly foamy. Salt and pepper to taste and set aside.

Remove the potatoes from the skillet; set aside. Sauté the onions until they are soft and set aside.

Add the potatoes and the onions to the beaten eggs and mix until they are completely covered by the eggs. Heat 3 tablespoons of the oil in a 10-inch skillet until very hot. Add the egg mixture and rapidly spread it out in the skillet. Lower the heat to medium and shake the pan briskly to prevent sticking.

When the potatoes begin to brown, slide the omelet out of the pan onto a platter. Place another platter on top of the omelet, and flip. Add the remaining 3 tablespoons oil to the pan and slide the omelet back into the skillet to brown on the other side. Repeat this process one more time and transfer to a serving platter. Sprinkle with the chopped parsley and serve at room temperature.

Poultry / Aves

CHICKEN AND ALMONDS
POLLO CON ALMENDRAS

This is one of my favorite recipes from my TV series. It is one of the truly classic recipes of Spain with sherry from the south, walnuts from the north, almonds from the Moorish conquerors, and chicken from the backyard. This dish is simple and exotic. Maybe that's why it's so much fun to make. You'll see for yourself, I'm sure. Or you can watch me on TV.

SERVES 4

3	tablespoons olive oil
2½	pounds chicken, cut into serving pieces
	Salt to taste
	Freshly ground pepper
	Flour for dusting
2	cloves garlic, mashed
1	medium chopped onion
2	tablespoons chopped flat parsley
1	cup chicken broth
5	walnuts, shelled
10	roasted almonds
1	large hard-boiled egg yolk
6	tablespoons (3 oz.) dry sherry
2	tablespoons chopped parsley for garnish

Sprinkle the chicken with salt and pepper and dust with flour.

In a large deep skillet, heat the oil and sauté the chicken for about 5 minutes or until golden on all sides. Remove to a warm platter.

In the same skillet, sauté the garlic, onion, and flat parsley until onion is soft.

Return the chicken to the skillet and add the broth. Salt and pepper to taste and mix well. Cover and cook over low heat for about 30 minutes or until chicken is tender.

In a food processor or blender, add the walnuts, almonds, egg yolk, and the sherry and blend until smooth. Pour the mixture over the chicken, mix well, and continue cooking for about 10 more minutes or until the chicken is done. Transfer the chicken and mixture to a serving platter and garnish with the chopped parsley.

This dish teams beautifully with my Cucumber Salad and Saffron Rice.

Meat / Carnes

PORK LOIN IN ORANGE LIQUEUR
CERDO A LA NARANJA

Imagine all the flavor and hearty pleasure of a crusty, juicy roast loin of pork. Now add the excitement of orange liqueur, the sweetness of orange juice, and the tang of garlic and spice, roasted to a crisp glaze. Olé milagro: You are making magic in your oven.

SERVES 4-6

MARINADE
- ¼ cup chopped onion
- 4 cloves garlic, peeled
- ¼ cup (2 oz.) dry white wine
- 1 teaspoon lemon juice
- ½ cup freshly squeezed orange juice
- ¼ cup (2 oz.) Cointreau liqueur

1	teaspoon salt (or less)
¾	cup olive oil
1	pork loin (about 3 lb., boned and trimmed)
1	small orange, peeled, sliced, and slices cut into halves
1	small onion, peeled, sliced, and slices cut into halves
6	sprigs parsley for garnish

In a food processor or blender, mix all the ingredients for the marinade. Blend well until smooth.

Cut a pocket about ¾ way deep along the length of the roast and rub the inside and outside with the marinade. Insert the orange slices and onion slices along the inside of the pocket and tie it up with a string.

Place the roast in a shallow flat bowl and pour the rest of the marinade over it. Marinate for about 1 hour, refrigerated, rolling the roast from time to time to coat it well with the marinade. Drain and reserve the marinade for later use.

Place the roast in a baking pan with a rack and bake in a 325°F preheated oven for about 1¾ hours, basting with the reserved marinade every 20 minutes.

Remove the roast to a serving platter, pour some of the reserved marinade over it, and garnish the sides of the roast with the parsley sprigs.

You will add to the pleasure of this dish by serving Potatoes in Paprika Sauce and a fresh green salad.

VEAL CUTLETS WITH TOMATO AND CILANTRO
TERNERA CON TOMATE Y CILANTRO

There's a Spanish restaurant in Chicago called La Paella. I tried this dish and loved the spicy, flavorful sauce poured over the tender, breaded cutlets. The cilantro imparts a piquancy that contrasts with the delicate veal. That's my touch, of course.

SERVES 4

SEASONING MIXTURE

2	cloves garlic, peeled
1	tablespoon chopped fresh cilantro
1	teaspoon red wine vinegar
⅛	teaspoon freshly ground pepper

½   teaspoon salt (or less)
3   tablespoons olive oil
1   pound veal cutlets, cut into 4 servings
3   eggs, lightly beaten, or egg substitute equivalent
1   cup cracker or bread crumbs
½   cup olive oil
½   pound onion, peeled and sliced
2   tablespoons chopped fresh cilantro
2   cups canned crushed tomatoes
     Salt to taste
3   orange slices for garnish
2   sprigs parsley for garnish

In a food processor or blender, mix all the ingredients for the seasoning mixture and blend until smooth.

Rub the seasoning into the meat. Then dip the meat slices, one at a time, into the beaten egg and then coat with the cracker crumbs. Refrigerate meat for about 15 minutes.

In a large skillet, heat the oil over medium heat and fry the veal on both sides until golden. Arrange the veal on a serving platter and keep warm.

In the same skillet, sauté the onion and cilantro until onion is soft. Add the tomatoes and salt to taste. Cook, uncovered, over medium heat until half of the liquid is evaporated.

Pour the mixture over the veal and garnish with the orange slices and parsley sprigs.

Serve this dish with White Rice with Sherry or your favorite pasta.

Desserts / Postres

RUM CAKE
BIZCOCHO BORRACHO

Nobody makes a rum cake like my Aunt Noema. This is not an ordinary dessert. It is like a night on the town, and if you share it with someone you care about, this bizcocho de ron *will warm your lips and your heart. Ask Aunt Noema.*

SERVES 10

CAKE
- ¾ cup water
- ¾ cup corn oil
- ½ cup (4 oz.) dark rum
- 5 eggs, gently beaten
- 5 ounces vanilla instant pudding filling
- 24 ounces yellow cake mix
- ¾ cup chopped pecans or walnuts
- ½ cup melted butter

GLAZE
- ¼ cup water
- 3 tablespoons melted butter
- ¼ cup (2 oz.) dark rum
- ½ cup fine sugar

In a large bowl, gently mix all the ingredients for the cake except the nuts and the butter. Set aside.

Grease and flour a 9-inch tube pan. Sprinkle the nuts over the bottom and pour the ½ cup melted butter over them. Fold in the reserved cake mixture and bake in a 350°F preheated oven for about 35 minutes or until the top of the cake has turned golden. Remove from oven. When cake is cool, invert it onto a round serving tray.

In a small saucepan, combine all the ingredients for the glaze and bring to a boil for about 2 minutes, stirring constantly, or until the sugar is dissolved and the sauce has a smooth consistency. Pour the glaze over the cake in a thin stream, letting the glaze soak into the cake. Set aside for about 1 hour before serving. Serve at room temperature.

The Wall at Avila

OLD CASTILE

Old Castile is old castles and cathedrals. It is rich in mystical experience, and its deep roots in Catholic Christianity kept it from significant Arab influence from the south and Protestant influence from the north. It was from the northern Castilian city of Burgos that the holy warrior, El Cid, began his fanatical campaign against the Moorish caliphs. In the southern area of the region sits the city of Ávila, surrounded by thick walls and filled with churches and the massive mountain Cathedral of Ávila, which stands higher than any other in Europe. Ávila was the home of Saint Theresa, whose passionate faith and intellectual powers inspired the Catholic leaders of Spain in their campaign against the Protestant Reformation that spread throughout most of Europe.

Salamanca, in the western region, has one of Europe's great universities. Salamanca University was founded in 1218 and was the center of Spanish intellectual thought and scholarly renaissance. Columbus consulted with the Salamanca faculty astronomers, geographers, and philosophers seeking their advice and information to fortify his own theories before he set sail for the New World. Valladolid, an early capital of Spain, possesses another fine and historic university. The great cities of Castile—Alcázar, Burgos, Segovia, León, and San Vincente—contain great monuments of mortar and stone, enormous cathedrals, castles, and fortresses that sit in silent grandeur on the stony, forbidding hills. They are impenetrable guardians against outside forces that might have erased the character and spirit of this unique land.

Old Castile is yesterday today. Fairy-tale pinnacles and towers tell silent stories of long-haired princesses and royal warriors. The great Roman aqueduct that circles the ancient city of Segovia dominates the landscape and boggles the mind with wonder. The vaulted carved ceilings of the cathedrals and monasteries create heavenly spaces that house the spirits of holy people.

The Old Castilians, filled with piety and religious discipline, remained simple people of the land. Dominant kings and cardinals and harsh geography limited their access to outside cultural influences. Their home is a land of peasant villages with tiny hillside cottages of stone and whitewash. Some are burrowed into the earth like caves, private fortresses that have housed many generations. Old Castilians are personal survivors. Thousands of family gardens grow much of the local produce. Shepherds lead large flocks of sheep and goats, and small farms and rustic village *casitas* raise chickens, pigeons, and pigs. The backyard gardens and the family livestock are basic to the general Castilian cuisine.

Old Castile sets a basic table. Even many of the restaurants of the Old Castilian cities present hearty, wholesome food simply and proudly. The bread of Castile is brick-oven-baked, crusty and abundant. Stews made with all kinds of meat and vegetables are thick and irresistibly delicious. Roasting suckling pig, weighing no more than eight pounds, is a favorite. Careful roasting produces a tender meat so succulent it can be carved with the edge of a dinner plate. Roast lamb and grilled lamb chops are peasant staples. Small birds like pigeon, quail, and Cornish hen are regular kitchen fare. Tiny potatoes, sweet red peppers, asparagus, and fresh haricot beans are everyday dishes. Throughout the world these are the foods of luxury and the gourmet. Yet here, where the family table is the family wealth, the grand is simple. Old values remain unchanged for over 2,000 years.

Long before the castles and the convents of Old Castile were built and long, long before the kings and crusaders came, there was wine. Where the cold, wet Atlantic climate of the high north meets the hot, dry Mediterranean climate of the south is the great wine country of Old Castile. This endless, rolling land from the hills to the plains with its enormous abundance of grapes and bodegas is called the Rioja. Riverbanks are bordered by lush grapevines. In the spring when the blossoms are full and the breezes come down from the highlands crossing the plains, the petals and the leaves of the grapevines are carried to the water and create El Rio Hojas, Riojas, the river of leaves.

THE WINES OF OLD CASTILE

Rioja wines are different from other wines of the world. Most of the wine producers of any country today are moving full-speed ahead with the latest technology of vinification and techniques to hasten the aging process. (An economic necessity, perhaps, but a contradiction in terms, nevertheless.) Although some of the bodegas of Rioja are beginning to adopt modern winemaking practices, the overriding philosophy of Riojan winemaking is a careful, slow process of cultivation, blending, and aging. The Rioja Wine Control Board, in existence since 1560, established lengthy rules for all phases of the winemaking process. Its label on the back of all Rioja bottles is a guarantee of quality and origin.

During the middle of the nineteenth century when most of the French vineyards were wiped out by disease, the French winemakers came to Spain to reestablish themselves and renew their wine production. Although their influence made some impact on the Spanish wine industry of the time, it was the French who gained, taking root-stock and grape varieties back to France, leaving the vintners of Rioja with their classic techniques, unique climate, and very special grapes.

Three basic elements create the rare Rioja wine character: climate, grape variety, and the laborious, loving process of barrel aging. The combination of the Atlantic and Mediterranean weather patterns provides the perfect balance of moisture and sun during the summer with cold and protection during the winter. The varieties of grapes, each a perfect specimen of its kind, allow the bodega masters to blend outstanding wines to create a wonderfully varied spectrum of color, character, taste, perfume, and alcohol content. The aging process takes place in handmade barrels of American oak. The aging process is unhurried, peaceful, and protected. As long ago as the sixteenth century, laws were passed in Rioja to prevent heavy wagons and their draft-horse teams from lumbering loudly past bodegas to insure that the gentle aging process would continue undisturbed. The slow aging in oak barrels gives the Rioja wines their unusual "woody," earthy flavor. It is a taste with a gentle nose that speaks of a wine undiminished by anything less than the pure natural process.

The grapes of Rioja are seven: four black and three white. The black grapes are grown in the southern lands and produce the robust red wines. The northern white grapes thrive in the higher, cooler regions and produce excellent, fruity white wines and rosé blends.

Of the four black grapes, the Garnacha tinta are the most heavily cultivated. They are very fruity when young and high in alcohol, do not age well, and are basically used for blending the lighter rosés.

The Tempranillo is the most outstanding of the black grapes. It creates a beautifully balanced, robust, and fruity wine. It resists oxidation and develops tastefully with long aging.

The Mazuelo is a gentle, fragile grape similar to several fine French varieties. It has little aroma but a refreshing flavor and blends well with the other wines of age.

Graciano is a traditional Riojan grape with many outstanding qualities. Although Graciano is low in alcohol, this black, thin-skinned small grape yields a wine that tastes fresh and fruity and adds fragrance to the wines it is blended with.

The white wines of Rioja include the Viura, which produces a fruity, fragrant wine. When added to Tempranillo it creates an excellent *clarete*, a light red wine.

Malvasia grows in the northern high country and yields a bitter-sweet, golden pressing. The Malvasia is often combined with Viura wine to produce a very full-flavored, dominant white Rioja.

Garnacha blanca is a third white grape that has limited application. It produces a fresh, high-alcohol wine with a sweet taste. It is cold pressed, unaged, and serves the domestic market very well.

Rioja wines are becoming high-demand products with characteristics rivaling the more highly publicized Burgundies and Bordeaux, which are actually less aged and higher priced. With some investigation and dedication to the task, the purchase and building of a cellar of Rioja wines will reward you many times over. They are the most carefully aged and blended wines in the world and keep well for decades. *Excellent* and *Very Good* vintage years are available five out of every ten years, which is a remarkable achievement in the world of wines.

The full character and completion of a classic Spanish meal can only be achieved in the company of an honest, soulful Spanish wine, the best of which says Rioja.

Appetizers / Tapas

MUSHROOMS SEGOVIA
SETAS ESTILO SEGOVIA

You're making a special Spanish dinner and you're almost out of time and ideas. Try this classic Castilian favorite. The sizzle of the chorizo dancing with the subtle texture of the mushrooms will awaken the taste buds and enhance your guests' appetites. And you can create this wonderful dish in less than 10 minutes.

SERVES 4

1	tablespoon olive oil
2	tablespoons butter (or less)
¾	pound small mushrooms, caps only
2	ounces (¼ cup) chopped chorizo
2	cloves garlic, peeled
2	tablespoons chopped fresh cilantro
¼	cup (2 oz.) dry white wine
	Salt to taste
	Freshly ground pepper
2	sprigs parsley for garnish

In a large skillet, heat the oil and butter and sauté the mushrooms, shaking the pan briskly, for about 2 minutes. Add the chorizo, garlic, and cilantro and continue cooking uncovered over high heat for about 2 minutes more. Add the wine, salt and pepper to taste, and mix well. Continue cooking until wine evaporates. Remove and discard the garlic cloves.

Transfer the mixture to a serving platter and garnish with parsley sprigs.

CHEESE BALLS STUFFED WITH OLIVES
RELLENO DE ACEITUNAS (BOLITAS)

This is really fun food. The bolitas are fun to make, fun to serve, and definitely fun to eat. From the crispy crust to the sweet pimento stuffing, this delightful dish will surely please everyone.

SERVES 4

1	cup shredded sharp cheddar cheese
¼	teaspoon paprika
2	teaspoons butter
½	cup flour
25	stuffed small olives, rinsed and drained

In a food processor or blender, mix all the ingredients except the olives and blend until smooth.

Place one teaspoon of the mixture over each olive and shape it into a ball by rolling it with the palm of your hand. Repeat the process until all the olives have been rolled.

Place the olives in a greased or oiled baking pan and bake in a 400°F preheated oven for about 15 minutes.

Remove to a serving platter and serve at room temperature.

Vegetables / Legumbres

POTATOES IN VINEGAR SAUCE
PATATAS EN VINAGRETA

Whether they come in pink, white, blue, or red color skins, these tiny grade "B" potatoes become a wonderfully delicious vegetable. If low fat is a concern, place the marinated potatoes in a roasting pan and roast at 400°F for 15 minutes instead of sautéing. Either way, this dish is a wonder.

2   tablespoons olive oil
2   tablespoons butter
20   tiny new potatoes, blanched and dried off

DRESSING
2   cloves garlic, peeled
½   teaspoon salt (or less)
¼   teaspoon freshly ground pepper
1   teaspoon chopped flat parsley
½   teaspoon Dijon-style mustard
¼   cup red wine vinegar
½   cup olive oil
3   orange slices for garnish

In a large covered skillet, heat the 2 tablespoons of olive oil and the butter and sauté the potatoes, shaking the pan briskly, until they are tender. Remove the potatoes to a large mixing bowl and set aside.

In a food processor or blender, mix the garlic, salt, pepper, parsley, mustard, vinegar, and olive oil and blend until smooth.

Pour the blender mixture over the potatoes and mix well. Transfer the potato mixture to a serving platter and garnish with orange slices.

MIXED VEGETABLES, CASTILE STYLE
MENESTRA A LA CASTILLA

Remember when your mother said, "Eat your vegetables," and you didn't? Well, if she had made this vegetable dish you would have eaten them all . . . and asked for more. I mean, my children would ask for more just to see Mom set the pan on fire.

3   tablespoons olive oil
2   tablespoons butter (or less)
2   cloves garlic, mashed
¼   cup chopped serrano or prosciutto ham
1   small onion, peeled and sliced
2   carrots, peeled and thinly sliced
1   cup sliced mushrooms
1   head broccoli, separated into florets

2   red bell peppers, seeded and coarsely chopped
¼   teaspoon salt
    Freshly ground pepper
2   tablespoons (1 oz.) dry sherry
2   tablespoons (1 oz.) brandy
    Grated Parmesan cheese (optional)

In a large skillet, heat the oil and butter and sauté the garlic, ham, and onion until onion is soft. Add the carrots, mushrooms, broccoli, salt, and pepper and sauté over high heat, shaking the pan briskly, until vegetables are almost tender. Add the sherry and brandy and flambé (be very careful) until flames subside.

Remove to a serving platter, sprinkle with Parmesan cheese, and serve hot.

CHRISTMAS RED CABBAGE
LOMBARDA DE NAVIDAD

This is a typical dish prepared in my family household for the Christmas holiday. It is highly nutritious, easy to prepare, and it will change all your ideas about how cabbage is supposed to taste. Feliz Navidad.

SERVES 4 – 6

5   tablespoons butter
2   medium onions, peeled and thinly sliced
2   cloves garlic, peeled and mashed
1   small head red cabbage, shredded
3   red apples, peeled, cored, and cubed
½   pound cubed serrano or prosciutto ham
½   cup wine vinegar
2   cups water
2   bay leaves, crumbled
3   medium white boiling potatoes, peeled and cubed
1   teaspoon salt (or less)
¼   teaspoon freshly ground pepper
4   orange slices for garnish
2   sprigs parsley for garnish

In a large casserole, heat the butter and sauté the onion and garlic until onion is soft. Add the cabbage, apples, and ham and cook uncovered over medium-low heat, stirring occasionally, for about 5 minutes or until cabbage starts to soften. Add the vinegar, water, bay leaves, potatoes, salt, and pepper and bring to a boil. Cover and cook over low heat for about one hour. Mix well and remove to a serving platter.

Garnish with orange slices and parsley and enjoy the holidays.

Fish / Pescado

DRIED COD RIOJA STYLE
BACALAO ESTILO RIOJA

This is a stove-top recipe that tastes like it's been cooked for hours under slow heat. I got it from my Aunt Luz Delia, who likes to cook simple, fast, and very delicious dishes. This one comes from the old country where wine is cooked with almost everything. The white wine in this recipe creates a flavor that takes you out of the fish market and into the bodegas of old Spain.

SERVES 4

1	pound salted dried cod fillets, skinned and boned
3	tablespoons olive oil
4	cloves garlic, mashed
2	medium onions, peeled and sliced
¾	cup tomato sauce
½	cup (4 oz.) dry white wine
2	canned pimentos, chopped
¼	cup small stuffed olives
¼	cup raisins, soaked in water and drained
1	bay leaf
½	pound (1 cup) cooked white cannellini beans
1	teaspoon capers
	Salt to taste
6	lemon slices for garnish
3	sprigs parsley for garnish

Place the cod in a bowl of water and soak water overnight. Drain. Shred the cod with a fork and set aside.

In a large skillet, heat the olive oil and sauté the garlic and onion until onion is soft. Add the tomato sauce, wine, pimento, olives, raisins, and bay leaf and cook over medium-high heat, uncovered, for about 5 minutes, stirring to mix well. Add the beans, capers, cod, and salt to taste. Mix well. Cover and cook over low heat for about 20 minutes or until the cod is done. Discard bay leaf.

Remove to a serving platter and garnish with lemon slices and sprigs of parsley.

Serve this fish dish with Catalán Style Spinach and baked potato.

Poultry / Aves

STUFFED CORNISH HENS RIOJA STYLE
CORNISH A LA RIOJANA

This recipe has everything. The tiny Cornish hens are poached until they're plump with meat, raisins, red wine, butter, onions, garlic, bread crumbs, milk, and honey. It's a whole meal on wings. And it's classic Spanish.

SERVES 4

4	Cornish hens, washed and dried
½	cup raisins
¼	cup (2 oz.) red wine
5	tablespoons butter (or less)
¼	cup chopped onion
2	tablespoons chopped serrano or prosciutto ham
2	cloves garlic, peeled and mashed
1½	cups cooked rice
2	cups bread crumbs
1½	cups milk
½	teaspoon salt (or less)
	Flour for dusting
8	orange slices for garnish

DRESSING

2	cloves garlic
3	tablespoons chopped onion
2	teaspoons red wine vinegar
½	teaspoon salt (or less)
1	tablespoon melted butter (or less)
1	tablespoon honey
¾	cup olive oil

In a small bowl, soak the raisins in the wine and set aside.

In a large skillet, heat the 5 tablespoons butter and sauté the onion, ham, and garlic until onion is soft. Add the raisins and wine and cook over high heat for about 1 minute. Remove the mixture from the skillet to a large bowl and add the cooked rice, bread crumbs, milk, and salt. Mix well and set aside.

In a food processor or blender, mix all the ingredients for the dressing. Blend until smooth and set aside.

Stuff the birds with the mixture from the large bowl, then brush the birds with the blender dressing and coat with flour. Close the cavity with small skewers and place the birds in an oiled or buttered baking pan. Bake in a 350° F preheated oven for about one hour, brushing with the dressing every 20 minutes, until birds are done.

Remove to a serving platter and garnish with the orange slices.

These hens are best served with a green, leafy salad and a bottle of Rioja wine.

CHICKEN WITH TOMATO AND HAM
POLLO A LA CASTILLANA

Chicken is a common dish until you cook it like this. The numerous ingredients including herbs, spices, fruit, meat, and wine create a banquet of flavors. But don't worry about all the ingredients. The cooking is simple.

SERVES 4

4	tablespoons olive oil
2½	pounds chicken pieces, washed and dried
2	cloves garlic, peeled and mashed

   1 tablespoon chopped salt pork
   1 medium onion, peeled and chopped
   2 tablespoons chopped serrano or prosciutto ham
   3 tablespoons chopped fresh cilantro
   1 cup canned whole tomatoes, drained and chopped
  ¼ cup raisins
   2 crumbled bay leaves
  ½ cup chicken broth
  ½ cup (4 oz.) dry white wine
  16 small stuffed olives, washed and drained
   6 seedless dried prunes
  1½ teaspoons salt
      Freshly ground pepper
   6 orange slices for garnish
   3 sprigs parsley for garnish

In a large skillet, heat the oil and sauté the chicken until golden. Set aside.

In the same skillet, sauté the garlic, salt pork, onion, ham, and cilantro until onion is soft. Return the chicken to the skillet and add the tomatoes, raisins, bay leaves, chicken broth, wine, olives, prunes, and salt and pepper to taste. Mix well.

Cook uncovered over medium-high heat for about 15 minutes and mix well.

Cover and cook over low heat for about 20 minutes more or until the chicken is tender.

Remove to a serving platter and garnish with the orange slices and the parsley sprigs.

Serve with a Spanish rice dish.

CHICKEN IN CHORIZO AND PIMENTO SAUCE
POLLO A LA RIOJANA

Chicken is just chicken until a traditional recipe like this one turns it into a comida especial. The tang of the chorizo with the sweetness of the pimento creates a combination of tastes you don't find when chicken is just chicken.

3	cloves garlic, peeled
1	medium onion, peeled and chopped
1	chorizo, skinned and chopped
1	canned whole pimento, drained and chopped
3	tablespoons chopped fresh cilantro
7	tablespoons olive oil
½	teaspoon salt (or less)
1	tablespoon cornstarch
1	cup chicken broth
2	large skinless whole chicken breasts, split in half to make 4 portions
	Freshly ground pepper
	Flour for dusting
6	lemon slices for garnish
3	sprigs parsley for garnish

In a food processor or blender, mix the garlic, onion, chorizo, pimento, cilantro, 3 tablespoons of olive oil, salt, and cornstarch. Blend until smooth. With the motor running, add the broth in a thin stream until smooth. Set aside.

Sprinkle the chicken with salt and pepper and dust with flour.

In a large skillet, heat the remaining oil and sauté the chicken on both sides until golden. Remove to a warm platter.

Wipe off the skillet and pour in the reserved blender mixture. Cook uncovered over medium heat for about 5 minutes, mixing occasionally until sauce thickens.

Return the chicken to the skillet and cover with the sauce. Cover and cook over low heat for about 20 minutes or until the chicken is tender. Remove the chicken to a serving platter. Mix the sauce in the skillet well and pour over the chicken. Garnish with lemon slices and sprigs of parsley.

Serve this with a side dish of White Rice and Sherry.

Meat / Carnes

PORK CHOPS RIOJA STYLE
CHULETAS A LA RIOJANA

Maybe you saw this recipe on TV. Maybe it went too fast to remember. Maybe the phone rang. Well, here it is again. Take your time. Prepare this dish carefully and take a little time out for a sip or two of the fresh Rioja red wine. Ahhh. Now you have something great from Spain's "river of leaves."

SERVES 4

4	6 oz. center-cut pork chops about 1 inch thick
	Salt to taste
	Freshly ground pepper
3	tablespoons olive oil
3	cloves garlic, mashed
1	large onion, chopped
¼	cup chopped chorizo
2	tablespoons chopped fresh cilantro
2	medium tomatoes, chopped
3	pimentos, canned, coarsely chopped
½	cup (4 oz.) red wine
2	sprigs parsley for garnish
3	orange slices for garnish

Sprinkle the chops with salt and pepper and set aside.

In a large skillet, heat the oil and sauté the pork chops on both sides until lightly golden. Remove to a warm platter.

In the same skillet, sauté the garlic, onion, chorizo, and cilantro until onion is soft. Return the pork chops to the skillet and add the tomatoes, pimento, wine, and salt and pepper to taste. Cover and cook over medium heat for about 15 minutes or until the pork chops are done.

Remove the pork chops and mixture to a serving platter and garnish with the parsley and orange slices.

Serve this dish with Green Beans and Potatoes.

HAM WITH ORANGE SAUCE
JAMÓN A LA NARANJA

In between the cathedrals, castles, and mountains of Segovia is the restaurant Hosteria Pintor Zuloaga. This particular dish comes from this charming four-fork restaurant. Locally produced ham and fresh oranges create this maravilloso *meat dish. I use mandarin oranges for added zest. You can create the same sensation in your own kitchen, and, who knows, maybe you'll get four forks, too.*

SERVES 4

1	can (11 oz.) mandarin oranges
¼	cup brown sugar
½	cup (4 oz.) red wine
2	tablespoons olive oil
3	pounds cooked boneless ham
2	orange slices for garnish

In a food processor or blender, mix all the ingredients except the ham and orange garnish. Blend until smooth.

Place the ham in an oiled or buttered baking pan and pour the mixture over the ham. Bake in a 375° F preheated oven for about 15 minutes, basting frequently with the sauce.

Remove the ham to a serving platter and pour some of the sauce over it. Garnish with the orange slices.

Serve with fresh steamed broccoli and a simple rice dish.

SLICED BEEF AND POTATOES
PICADILLO

This is my version of a traditional Castilian recipe. Use new potatoes and slice the beef very, very thin so it cooks quickly and seals in the juice. When you flambé the wine and brandy, the meat absorbs all the flavor and creates a simple meal with gourmet appeal.

SERVES 4

1½	pounds beef steak, cut into very thin slices
	Salt to taste
	Freshly ground pepper

1   teaspoon paprika
5   tablespoons olive oil
3   cloves garlic, mashed
2   tablespoons chopped fresh cilantro
16 very small new potatoes, scrubbed and blanched
¼   cup (2 oz.) red wine
2   tablespoons (1 oz.) brandy
2   tablespoons chopped pimento for garnish
2   sprigs parsley for garnish

Sprinkle the meat with salt, pepper, and paprika; rub well and set aside.

In a large skillet, heat 3 tablespoons of the oil and sauté the garlic, cilantro, and the meat slices for about 5 minutes, shaking the pan briskly, until the meat turns brown. Remove the meat to a warm platter and set aside.

In the same skillet, add the remaining oil and sauté the potatoes, shaking the pan briskly, for about 5 minutes. Return the meat to the skillet and check for seasonings. Add the wine and brandy and flambé (being very careful) until flames subside. Cover and cook over low heat for about 5–10 minutes or until the potatoes are done.

Remove to a serving platter and garnish with the chopped pimentos and parsley sprigs.

Serve this dish with a salad of Escarole with Olives and Cheese and hot, crunchy bread.

Desserts / Postres

COFFEE AND WALNUT COOKIES
POSTRE DE CAFÉ Y ALMENDRAS

These are mucho *fast cookies with simple ingredients and only 15 minutes baking time. Make plenty because you'll eat every one.*

SERVES 6

2   beaten egg whites
¼   cup chopped walnuts

    1   teaspoon vanilla extract
 1⅓   cups fine sugar
    2   teaspoons instant coffee
   ⅛   teaspoon salt

In a mixing bowl, combine the sugar, coffee, and salt. Slowly add the egg whites while beating with a whisk until the mixture is smooth. Add the walnuts and the vanilla and mix well; set aside.

Place the mixture, one tablespoon at a time, on a buttered cookie sheet. Bake in a 325° F preheated oven for about 15 minutes or until the cookies are fully risen. Remove and let cool at room temperature before serving.

The Cathedral at Santiago de Compostela

GALICIA

Galicia is different from the rest of Spain. It represents the Celtic part of the Celtic-Iberian culture that evolved into modern Spain. As the Celts moved westward across Spain to their eventual homelands in Scotland and Ireland, they created a unique society in the coastal mountains of the northernmost part of Spain. Galicia is bordered to the south by Portugal; the special language of the Galicians, *Gallego*, is similar to Portuguese. Although the Celtic influence is evident in costume, conversation, and attitude, it is religion and geography that have done most to shape the character of the region.

Sometime in the ninth century, the supposed remains of St. James the Apostle were found in the area of Compostela. A great cathedral was built to glorify and house the sacred relic. The pope declared absolution from all sins to anyone who made the journey to Compostela to pay homage to the saint. The industrious monks of southern France and northern Spain built way-steps along the route to help the pilgrims make the journey. Routes were soon established from points throughout Europe, and a steady flow of penitents brought to Galicia a broad spectrum of cultural, culinary, and Christian elements. The Christian influence was so powerful in the region that the Moorish invaders never established themselves in Galicia; the region bears no marks of the Arab occupation of Spain.

Nature, however, has definitely left its mark. Galicia is beautiful, majestic, clean, and bountiful. Wild life flourishes and food is abundant. The mountains are split with deep ravines, much like the fjords of Norway, which carry clear, pure water down to the sea. The river ravines, the ocean, the northern bay, and the quiet coves along the rocky coast are filled with seafood of all description. Long, wet springtimes encourage lush pasturelands that support herds of cattle, sheep, goats, and game. Some of the best Spanish cheeses come from Galicia.

111

The moderate climate, though short on summer, allows all kinds of fruit and produce to grow abundantly. Galicians enjoy everything from exotic fruits to easily grown greens and beans.

Above all, it is the seafood that dominates. A sizable industry exists to harvest oysters and mussels from the unpolluted coves of the western shores. Scallops are a regional main event, most often stuffed and baked and served in their shells. Squid and octopus abound with classic culinary recipes so imaginative and tasty that they will change any squeamish ideas you may have about this sort of food. All varieties of shellfish are available: baked, broiled, steamed, cooked *cazuela* (stewpot) style, always surrounded with garden vegetables and accompanied by hearty broths and soups that warm the Galicians through many months of damp, drizzly days.

Greens are a major part of the Galician meal, including collards, kale, turnip tops, escarole, and cabbage. Hearty vegetables like potatoes, turnips, leeks, onions, and beans of all kinds are plentiful and are perfect additions to popular seafood soups and meat stews.

The Galician cuisine is just plain delicious. The recipes are basically simple but unusual, highlighting the beautiful flavors of foods that thrive in an unspoiled and unpolluted environment. The region bestows a natural bounty on those hardy souls who choose to live between the mountains and the sea.

THE WINES OF GALICIA

Galician wines are for Galicians. Most of the local wine is produced from white grapes that yield a dry, flowery taste. The red wines are robust, dry, and tart. All the wines have high alcohol content; numerous stories tell of incapacitated armies discombobulated by Galician drink. Many small, individually operated bodegas produce some excellent wines full of character and fine flavor. There is an outstanding white wine of the region, sometimes described as a light, delicate Moselle, which leaves a bubbly sensation on the palate. These wines are rare products of careful hands-on winemaking, but they never leave the region. They are much sought after by the local restaurants and citizens.

One of the wines that has made its way out of Galicia is the two-fisted, spellbinding, deceptively mild *aguardiente*. It is distilled from the skins and the pulp of the local grapes and cannot be easily drunk by itself. *Aguardiente* is poured, enflamed (to burn off some of the alcohol), and then drunk. (The liquid, by the way, does not heat up when ignited.) An ingredient in many Spanish recipes, *aguardiente* adds a piquancy not found in any other national cuisine.

Appetizers / Tapas

TUNA AND SCALLIONS CANAPE
ATÚN Y CEBOLLETAS

If anyone knows tuna it is the Galicians. They live by the sea and from the sea. Tuna is abundant, and this simple little tapas is just one of the ways Galicians enjoy this fish. Imagine a 150-pound tuna turning up on your cracker!

SERVES 4–7

14   ounces light tuna in water, drained and chopped
3   tablespoons mayonnaise
2   tablespoons sherry wine vinegar
1   tablespoon Tabasco sauce
5   small stuffed olives, finely chopped
2   tablespoons finely chopped scallions
1   tablespoon virgin olive oil
    Salt to taste
    Wheat crackers
    Pimento pieces for garnish

In a mixing bowl, combine all the ingredients except the crackers and pimento. Blend well. Place 1 tablespoon of the mixture on top of each cracker and garnish with a piece of pimento.

BAKED CLAMS AND CHORIZO
ALMEJAS CON CHORIZO

In Barcelona there is a Galician restaurant, Botafumeiro, where they serve an unusual appetizer, a combination of tender sweet clams and sizzling, spicy sausage baked to warm your heart and your body. It was created in the mountainside coastal villages of Galicia, where the summers are short and the food is pure and muy bonito.

SERVES 4

20   small littleneck clams
2   cups rock salt (about ½ inch deep in pan)
2   chorizos, skinned and finely chopped
1   clove garlic, peeled and mashed
2–3   drops Tabasco sauce
2   tablespoons dry sherry
Salt to taste
2   tablespoons chopped fresh parsley for garnish

Open clams and drain the liquid into a small bowl. Discard half of the shells. Place remaining shells with the meat in a baking dish that has been spread with rock salt about ½ inch thick. Set aside.

In a medium skillet, sauté the chorizo until crisp. Remove with a slotted spoon onto paper towels and set aside.

Combine the liquid from the clams with the garlic, Tabasco, wine, and salt. Mix well. Spoon the mixture into the clam shells and top with the reserved chopped chorizo.

Bake in a 400° F preheated oven for about 10 minutes or until the clam meat is tender (do not overcook).

Remove clams to a serving platter and garnish with chopped parsley.

Soups / Sopas

SEAFOOD SOUP GALICIAN STYLE
CALDERETA A LA GALICIANA

You could not create a seafood soup more typical of a Galician seaside village. It's a little like a bouillabaisse but with a touch more spice—and, of course, to make it truly Spanish, sherry and brandy. ¡A la salud!

SERVES 4

6	cups fish broth
½	teaspoon crumbled saffron
⅓	cup dry sherry
1	tablespoon brandy
2	tablespoons olive oil
1	bay leaf, crumbled
3	tablespoons chopped fresh cilantro
3	cloves garlic, chopped
1	large Spanish or Bermuda onion, peeled and chopped
1	pound fresh cod fillet, cut into 1-inch chunks
½	pound medium shrimp, shelled
¼	teaspoon freshly ground pepper
	Salt to taste
4	slices toasted French bread
½	teaspoon paprika

In a large casserole, combine all the ingredients except the bread and paprika. Bring to a boil. Cover and cook over low heat for about 20 minutes or until the fish is done.

Transfer the soup to individual soup bowls or crocks and top each with a slice of toast. Sprinkle the toast with the paprika and serve hot.

HAM AND CABBAGE SOUP
CALDO GALLEGO

This tastes like my grandmother's old-fashioned cooking. She got the recipe from her grandmother. Nothing lasts that long unless it's very special. This delicious combination of beans, meats, and vegetables tastes even better the next day, and the day after, and the day after that. Gracias, Grandma.

SERVES 4 – 5

½ pound small dried white Cannellini beans
8 cups water
2 tablespoons (1 oz.) brandy
2 ounces salted pork (optional)
2 pounds cured ham, diced
1 small hambone
3 chorizos, each cut into 4 pieces
1 medium onion, peeled and quartered
1 pound white potatoes, peeled and coarsely cubed
1 pound cabbage, coarsely chopped
1 pound parsnips, cut into chunks
   Salt to taste
   Freshly ground pepper
2 scallions (green part only), chopped, for garnish

Soak the beans in 5 cups water for about 12 hours. Drain, rinse, and set aside.

In a large casserole, add 8 cups water, brandy, reserved beans, salted pork, hambone, chorizo, and onion. Bring to a boil. Cover and cook over low heat (skimming the foam occasionally with a skimmer) for about 1 hour. Add the potatoes, cabbage, parsnips, and salt and pepper to taste. Mix well and bring to a boil. Cover partially and cook over low heat for about 30 minutes. Discard the bone and salted pork. Remove cover and continue cooking over low heat for about 30 minutes more.

Serve in individual soup bowls, garnished with the chopped scallions.

Egg Dishes / Tortillas

SHRIMP AND WINE OMELET
TORTILLA DE GAMBAS Y VINO BLANCO

In Mexico a thin flour or corn pancake is called a tortilla. *In Spain a* tortilla *is a combination of eggs whipped into an omelet, filled with peppers, onions, and spices and turned over once in the pan. It is an Old World/New World difference. I say make the Spanish* tortilla, *cut it in slices, and roll it up in a Mexican* tortilla. *That way you have the best of both worlds.*

SERVES 4

 4   eggs, slightly beaten, or egg substitute equivalent
 2   tablespoons (1 oz.) dry white wine
 ¾   cup chopped cooked shrimp
 3   tablespoons chopped green bell peppers
 ¼   cup finely chopped onions
     Salt to taste
     Freshly ground pepper
 ¼   cup butter
 1   tablespoon chopped parsley for garnish

In a mixing bowl, combine all the ingredients except the butter and the garnish. Blend well.

In a large skillet, heat the butter and pour the egg mixture evenly into the pan until it starts to turn golden on the bottom. Cover and cook over low heat until eggs are set. Shake the pan briskly and remove the omelet to a serving platter. Garnish with the chopped parsley and serve.

Shellfish / Mariscos

SCALLOPS IN WINE SAUCE
VIEIRAS EN SALSA DE VINO

The Galicians make a hearty wine that never leaves the region. The Galicians keep it to themselves, and what they don't drink they add to their endless seafood recipes. This is one of them. So sauté the scallops, uncork the wine and pour it on. Now you're eating Galiciana.

SERVES 4

¼	cup olive oil
¼	cup butter (or less)
4	cloves garlic, peeled and mashed
2	tablespoons chopped fresh cilantro
1	teaspoon paprika
1½	pounds sea scallops
¼	cup (2 oz.) dry white wine
½	cup heavy cream
	Salt to taste
	Freshly ground pepper
2	tablespoons scallions (green part only), chopped, for garnish

In a large skillet, heat the oil and butter over medium heat and sauté the garlic, cilantro, and paprika until garlic starts to sizzle. Add the scallops and wine. Sauté, shaking the pan briskly and mixing until scallops begin to cook. Add the cream, and salt and pepper to taste. Mix well, cover, and cook over low heat for about 5 minutes or until the scallops are done. Mix well. Remove to a serving platter and garnish with the chopped scallions.

Serve with Saffron Rice and a leafy green vegetable such as kale.

BAKED LOBSTER WITH PIMENTOS
LANGOSTA A LA GALICIANA

The Botafumeiro Restaurant in Barcelona presents this Galician recipe as prepared by its chef, Mouche Neiras. I have created my own personal version of this dish, with a touch of Dijon mustard and white wine. I always pour a nice glass of wine when I make this dish and it always comes out muy sabroso.

SERVES 4

3	tablespoons butter (or less)
3	tablespoons olive oil
6	tablespoons flour
2	cups milk
2	canned whole pimentos, rinsed and chopped
1	clove garlic, peeled and mashed
2	tablespoons chopped onion
3	tablespoons dry white wine
½	teaspoon Dijon-style mustard
1¼	pounds lobster meat, cut into chunks
1	teaspoon salt (or less)
¼	cup seasoned bread crumbs
6	sprigs chopped parsley for garnish, or 3 tablespoons fresh parsley for garnish

In a large deep skillet, melt the butter and olive oil over medium heat. Add the flour and mix continuously until smooth. Pour in the milk; mix well for about 1 minute. Add the pimentos, garlic, onion, wine, mustard, and lobster. Mix well, bring to a boil, and cook until sauce begins to thicken. Transfer the lobster and mixture to an oiled or buttered baking pan. Sprinkle the bread crumbs on top and bake in a 475° F preheated oven for about 15 minutes or until the bread crumbs are golden. Serve in the baking pan. Sprinkle with chopped parsley.

Serve this lobster dish with baked potato and string beans.

Fish / Pescado

HAKE IN PAPRIKA AND WINE SAUCE
MERLUZA ESTILO GALICIA

My Aunt America (nice name, no?) brought me this recipe from her home in La Coruña, Galicia. I made this dish on my TV show. The secret is the paprika sauce. It is spicy without being hot and full of seafood flavor without tasting fishy.

SERVES 4

- ½   cup olive oil
- 2   medium baking potatoes, peeled and thinly sliced
- 2   cloves garlic, peeled
- ½   cup chopped onion
- 2   tablespoons chopped flat parsley
- ¼   cup (2 oz.) dry white wine
- ½   teaspoon dry oregano
- 1   bay leaf, crumbled
- 1   tablespoon paprika
- ½   teaspoon salt (or less)
- ¼   teaspoon freshly ground pepper
- 3   tablespoons olive oil
- 4   hake or fresh cod fillets, about 6 ounces each
- 4   lemon slices for garnish
- 2   sprigs parsley for garnish

In a large skillet, heat the oil and fry the potatoes a few at a time until they are just tender. Drain, cool, and reserve.

In a food processor or blender, mix the garlic, onion, flat parsley, wine, oregano, bay leaf, paprika, salt, pepper, and 3 tablespoons olive oil. Blend until smooth. Reserve.

Divide the potatoes into 4 small baking dishes and place a fish fillet on top of each. Pour some of the reserved mixture over each fillet and bake in a 325° F preheated oven for about 20 minutes or until fish is done. Garnish with the lemon and parsley.

Serve this fish dish with Mixed Vegetables, Castile Style.

Desserts / Postres

ALMOND FLAN
FLAN DE ALMENDRAS

Flan is the national dessert of Spain. If you can caramelize sugar, you can create many variations on this light dessert. So get your technique down and whip out flan desserts like this one. You'll satisfy everyone's sweet tooth and cut down on cakes, cookies, ice cream, and chocolate.

SERVES 4 – 6

1¾	cups sugar
1	tablespoon water
½	cup ground almonds
3	cups milk
1	teaspoon grated lemon peel
6	eggs
¼	teaspoon salt
½	cup chopped walnuts for garnish

Caramelize* a 9-inch round baking pan 3 inches deep (without the tube) with ¾ cup sugar and 1 tablespoon water. Cover the bottom and sides of the pan with the caramel and set aside.

In a food processor or blender, mix the rest of the ingredients except the walnuts and blend until smooth. Pour the mixture into the caramelized baking pan and place it in a larger pan containing 1 inch of water. Bake in a 350° F preheated oven for about 1 hour or until the top is set and golden. Remove the pan from the water and let cool. Place a large serving plate over the pan, flip over and remove pan. Garnish with chopped walnuts and serve chilled.

*Carmelize — dissolve the sugar by adding water very slowly over low heat until it turns a golden color.

The Peaks of Europe (streams)

ASTURIAS

Asturias is simple and peaceful country. With the sea to the north and surrounded by mountains, Asturias is the most naturally protected region in all of Spain. The reconquest of Spain began in Asturias with the forces of the Christian armies gathering in the hidden villages of the mountains. Small roads wind their way through picturesque villages and mountain vistas that are untouched by modern life. The sea, the meadows, and the difficult terrain have created an unhurried society that tends its flocks and orchards and goes down to the sea in small boats that bring in abundant fish of great variety.

The Asturian cuisine is basically vegetables and seafood. One of the most popular local dishes is made with a special white bean, *fabada*, sometimes called a butter bean. It is slowly simmered with chorizo and a local Asturian sausage. *Fabadas* are basic to several recipes. The resourceful Spanish cook combines them with shellfish, or bits of beef or pork to make wonderfully hearty stews. There are no limits to ways of preparing fish in Asturias. Fish is cooked with tomatoes, onions, peppers, and wonderfully Spanish *salsa verde* and *alioli*. Veal and beef are popular, but sausage is the favorite meat. Several local varieties are imaginative combinations of spices and other ingredients.

The thick meadows and sweet pasturelands yield high-quality dairy products, which the Asturians process into an array of cheeses that rival some of the best in Europe. The most famous variety is Cabrales-Picón, a blue-veined cheese made from a blend of milk from cows, sheep, and goats. Cabrales is dried over a wood fire, then stored in stilted wooden sheds to age. When the blue veins of mold appear, the cheese is wrapped in chestnut leaves and stored in natural caves until it reaches the perfect level of heavy aroma and sharp taste. Cabrales-Picón is best enjoyed fresh, while it is soft and creamy.

There are no grapes in Asturias. There are apples. Excellent crops

123

of many varieties find their way onto the tables and into the recipes of the Asturian people.

There is no wine in Asturias. There is *sidra*, a bubbly cider made from the apples that grow everywhere on the hillsides and rolling lands of the coastal area. *Sidra* has an alcohol content of 7 or 8 percent and a semisweet taste. It is a delicious table beverage and a great companion to meat and fish dishes. Much of it is exported, and *sidra* is available in most liquor stores. It makes a great addition to your collection of liquid refreshments.

Appetizers / Tapas

BLUE CHEESE AND SHRIMP
GAMBAS EN QUESO CABRALES

Once upon a time a young shepherd was having his lunch of cheese and bread near the mouth of a cave when a beautiful young Asturian lady came walking by. The young shepherd placed his cheese on the floor of the cave and followed the girl. Several weeks later he returned to the cave and saw the cheese he had left behind. Only now, the cheese had blue veins and a strong taste. Ever since, the Asturians have been ripening their cheese in caves and following pretty girls across the beautiful hillsides.

SERVES 4 – 6

    8   ounces Cabrales or Roquefort cheese
   ¼   cup finely chopped cooked shrimp
    3   ounces cream cheese
    3   tablespoons finely chopped onion
    1   tablespoon dry sherry
        Salt to taste
    2   tablespoons chopped parsley for garnish
        Crackers

In a mixing bowl, combine all the ingredients except the parsley and the crackers and blend well until smooth. Transfer the mixture to a serving bowl, garnish with the parsley, and arrange the crackers around the bowl.

Salads / Ensaladas

ASPARAGUS, TUNA, AND BLUE CHEESE SALAD
ENSALADA ASTURIANA

Everyone loves a new and exciting salad. This is one. Tender asparagus, high-protein tuna, and incredibly delicious Cabrales or blue cheese will give you a salad that's out of this world. In fact, the Romans called Asturias the "end of the world."

SERVES 4

- 2 cups shredded iceberg lettuce
- 4 large rings red bell pepper
- 7 ounces canned chunk light tuna in water, drained and shredded
- 8 canned white asparagus spears, cut into halves, or fresh asparagus tips, blanched
- 4 sprigs parsley for garnish
- 6–8 ounces Cabrales-Picón cheese (or substitute Roquefort or Gorgonzola)

DRESSING
- 1 small egg yolk
- 5 tablespoons chopped onion
- 3 tablespoons applesauce
- 1 tablespoon sherry wine vinegar
- 1 teaspoon salt
- ¼ teaspoon freshly ground pepper
- ½ cup olive oil

Divide the shredded lettuce among four individual salad plates. Place one red pepper ring over each portion of lettuce. Divide the tuna into four portions and place one portion inside each ring. Garnish each plate with 4 pieces of asparagus. Set aside. Crumble the cheese and sprinkle over the salad.

In a food processor or blender, mix all the ingredients for the dressing except the olive oil. Blend well. With the motor running, pour the oil in a thin stream until sauce is thick.

Pour some of the dressing over the salad and garnish with a parsley sprig.

Soups / Sopas

SAUSAGE AND HAM STEW
FABADA

Fabada *is Asturias: rustic, earthy, and traditional. It is the most famous dish of the region, and Asturians insist it can only be made with lima beans from the province. But I know better. You can make this recipe with beans from your local market, and I'll bet it will still be a true Asturian* Fabada.

SERVES 4

1	tablespoon olive oil
2	ounces cured salted pork, rinsed and chopped
6	chorizos, each cut into 4 pieces
1½	pounds smoked ham, coarsely chopped
2	large onions, peeled and chopped
6	cloves garlic, peeled and mashed
2	medium tomatoes, seeded and chopped
1	teaspoon paprika
5	cups water
1	cup (8 oz.) dry white wine
1	bay leaf
2	cups fresh or frozen large lima beans
¼	teaspoon saffron
2	whole cloves
	Salt to taste
4	sprigs parsley for garnish

In a large casserole, heat the oil and sauté the pork until it starts to color. Add the chorizos, ham, onion, and garlic and sauté until the onions are soft. Add the tomatoes, paprika, water, wine, bay leaf, lima beans, saffron, cloves, and salt to taste. Mix well and bring to a boil. Cover and cook over low heat (occasionally skimming off the foam with a skimmer) for about 1 hour or until the beans are soft.

Serve in individual soup bowls and garnish with a sprig of parsley.
Serve with egg noodles or flat wide pasta.

Fish / Pescado

BAKED HAKE AND SHRIMP IN HARD CIDER
MERLUZA Y GAMBAS EN SIDRA

No wine is produced in Asturias, but the best hard cider in Europe is. This naturally fermented clear apple juice gives the fish and shrimp a tangy champagne taste. So "pop" the cider and sit down to a wonderful meal.

SERVES 4

3	medium baking potatoes, peeled and thinly sliced
½	cup chicken broth
3	large cloves garlic, peeled
1	cup chopped onion
2	teaspoons paprika
2	cups clam broth
1	cup hard cider
2	tablespoons chopped flat parsley
1	bay leaf, crumbled
¼	teaspoon thyme
3	tablespoons flour
¼	teaspoon freshly ground pepper
	Salt to taste
¼	cup olive oil
4	hake or similar fish fillets (about 6–8 ounces each)
½	pound large shrimp in their shells
1	green apple, seeded and thinly sliced for garnish
4	sprigs parsley for garnish

Spread the potatoes in the bottom of an oiled or buttered baking pan and pour the chicken broth over them. Bake in a 350° F preheated oven for about 15 minutes; remove and set aside.

In a food processor or blender (in a few steps, if necessary), mix the garlic, onion, paprika, clam broth, cider, flat parsley, bay leaf, thyme, flour, pepper, and salt to taste. Add the olive oil and blend until smooth; reserve.

Sprinkle the fillets with salt on both sides and place them on top of the sliced potatoes. Pour the reserved mixture over the fillets and bury the shrimp in the sauce. Bake in a 350° F preheated oven for about 20 minutes or until the fish is done.

Remove the fillets to individual serving platters and place 3 to 4 shrimp on each. Pour some of the sauce over the shrimp and garnish with the apple slices and parsley sprigs.

Serve with Lima Beans and Saffron.

SCROD FILLET IN WHITE SAUCE
FILETE DE PESCADO EN SALSA BLANCA

In the inaccessible terrain of the Asturian mountains, the paradors are comfortable, hospitable places of rest. In the area of Gijon, the Parador Molino Viejo (The Old Windmill) specializes in native seafood dishes, including Scrod Fillet in White Sauce. This is my version.

SERVES 4

4	scrod fillets (about 6–8 ounces each)
	Salt and pepper to taste
	Flour for dusting
¼	cup melted butter
3	cloves garlic, peeled and mashed
¼	cup chopped onion
1	small bay leaf
1½	cups milk
2	tablespoons hard cider
1	teaspoon salt (or less)
1	tablespoon cornstarch
6	tablespoons olive oil
3	sprigs parsley for garnish

Sprinkle the fish with salt and pepper and dust with flour. Set aside.

In a medium saucepan, add the butter and sauté the garlic, onion, and bay leaf until onion is soft. Transfer the mixture to a food processor or blender. Add the milk, cider, salt to taste, and the cornstarch. Blend well until smooth. Transfer the mixture back to the saucepan and cook over medium heat, stirring constantly, until sauce is thickened. Remove, set aside, and keep warm.

In a large skillet, heat the oil and sauté the fish until golden on both sides and cooked through.

Remove to a serving platter. Mix the reserved sauce and pour over the fish. Garnish with the parsley sprigs and serve hot.

Pair this with Potatoes and Greens or Broccoli with Walnuts and Raisins.

Meat / Carnes

FILET MIGNON WITH HAM AND CHEESE SAUCE
ENTRECOTE CON JAMÓN Y QUESO

This recipe is for meat lovers. It calls for a hearty appetite, a fine Spanish wine for company, and a relaxing stroll after dinner.

SERVES 4

4   filet mignons (about 6–8 ounces each)
4   thin slices serrano or prosciutto ham
     Butter

SAUCE
3   tablespoons olive oil
4   ounces Cabrales or blue cheese at room temperature
3   tablespoons dry sherry
3   ounces cream cheese at room temperature
1   clove garlic, peeled and mashed
1   tablespoon finely chopped fresh cilantro

Cut a pocket along the side of each filet and insert a slice of ham in each. Place the meat in a broiler pan and dot with butter. Place under a broiler, turning once, until meat is cooked to your satisfaction.

Meanwhile, in a small saucepan, combine all the ingredients for the sauce. Cook over low heat, stirring constantly, until the sauce is smooth. Remove and set aside.

Place the filets on serving platters and pour some of the sauce over each.

Serve with a baked potato and a mixed green salad.

BUTTERFLY CHOPS IN APPLE CIDER
CHULETAS A LA SIDRA

At the restaurant Las Delícias in Gijon, chuletas are a specialty of the house. These stuffed pork loin chops are prepared in the traditional style. The applesauce and hard cider add a fruity taste to the seasoned meat. I, of course, have added my own touch of cilantro. I feel that skillet cooking instead of baking keeps the meat tender and jugoso.

SERVES 4

4	large center cut pork chops
	Salt to taste
	Freshly ground pepper
3	tablespoons butter
2	cloves garlic, peeled
¼	cup chopped onion
2	tablespoons chopped fresh cilantro
½	cup applesauce
1	cup hard cider
1	tablespoon cornstarch
2	tablespoons olive oil
3	orange slices for garnish
3	sprigs parsley for garnish

Cut a pocket sideways halfway through the pork chops and season with salt and pepper inside and out.

In a large skillet, heat the butter over medium heat and sauté the pork chops until lightly golden on both sides. Cover and cook over low heat for about 10 minutes.

Meanwhile, in a food processor or blender, mix the garlic, onion, cilantro, applesauce, cider, salt to taste, cornstarch, and olive oil. Blend until smooth.

Pour the sauce over the pork chops and continue cooking over low heat (covered) for about 15 minutes more or until the pork chops are tender. Arrange the chops on a serving platter. Mix the sauce well and pour over the chops. Garnish with the orange slices and the sprigs of parsley.

Serve this dish along with a leafy green vegetable.

Desserts / Postres

RICE PUDDING 43
PUDIN DE ARROZ 43

Licor 43 is a brilliant, clear golden liqueur with the unforgettable flavor of citrus fruits grown on the shores of the Mediterranean, delightfully balanced with the flavor of real vanilla. It has a soft aroma, delicate sweetness, incomparable sensuality, and a remarkable mixability. Licor 43 is a great ingredient to experiment with, so why not start with this traditional rice pudding recipe? I am sure it will become one of your favorite desserts to serve to friends.

SERVES 10

6	cups milk
1	teaspoon ground cinnamon
5	tablespoons Licor 43
3¾	cups cooked white rice
2	tablespoons melted butter
5	eggs, lightly beaten
2	cups fine sugar
¼	teaspoon salt (or less)
2	teaspoons vanilla extract
1½	cups raisins

In a large deep casserole, heat the milk, cinnamon, and Licor 43 over low heat for about 5 minutes. Add the rice and butter. Mix well and set aside.

In a medium bowl, mix the eggs, sugar, and salt until smooth. Add the egg mixture to the rice and mix well until thickened. Add the vanilla and raisins and mix until all ingredients are well blended.

Spread the mixture evenly in a buttered baking pan (9 x 13). Place the baking pan in a larger pan containing water to a depth of about 1 inch. Bake in a 350° F preheated oven for about 1 hour or until the liquid is evaporated. Remove.

Let cool. Serve chilled in individual dessert bowls.

San Sebastian

THE BASQUE COUNTRY

The Basque Country is the only region of Spain that is called a country. The official Spanish designation of the region is País Vasco. The origin of the Basque people is still a mystery. One of two popular theories considers the Basque people as the last survivors of the Celtic-Iberian culture who entrenched themselves between the tortuous Pyrenees to the northeast and the precipitous Atlantic coastline to the west. The other theory is based on a mass immigration from the northeast after a prehistoric cataclysmic disaster. Whatever their origin, the Basques have remained belligerently independent, hardy, and self-sufficient.

Much of their history is tied to the sea. Their ocean adventures in search of whales and cod took them to the northeast Canadian coastline long before Columbus discovered the Americas. Among the long list of Spanish sea heroes is the obscure Juan Sebastián Elano, a Basque explorer, who was actually the first sailor to circumnavigate the globe. Today the Basque engage in ship-building and commercial fishing, continuing their historic marriage to the sea.

Along the separatist Basque idea of being a country unto itself, the Basque people cling to their own language. It is a strange tongue without known roots or similarities to any other language patterns. The combination of geography, language, and fiercely independent attitude has insulated the Basque culture from outside influences. No invader has ever gained an advantage or foothold in the region. Charlemagne was defeated by the Basques in the Pyrenees near Roncaville. The Arthurian warrior Roland was killed in the same locale, a wild mountain area of dense forest and alternating hills of rock and sliding stone. Along the northern coastline the terrain softens and opens to a view of the magnificent Bay of Biscay and its long, curving beach, LaConcha. Facing the sea is the beautiful city of San Sebastián. Once the vacation land of the Spanish aristocracy, the city is a collection of beautiful old mansions, fine restaurants, hotels, and quaint shops. It is a seaside jewel about to reemerge as a major attraction for Europeans and world visitors as one secret of Basque life becomes known outside its borders. That secret is its cuisine.

Food is the passion of the people. While its history is filled with recipes of great abundance and feasting, the Basque Country is the birthplace of the modern culinary phenomenon *nouvelle cuisine*—an inspired decision to use simple cooking techniques to bring out the most natural flavors of the extraordinary seafood and fresh vegetables of the northern Spanish climate. Some of the restaurant fadists of New York, London, and Los Angeles have produced pale imitations of *nouvelle cuisine* and have replaced the exquisite with the dainty; the select with the meager; and artful presentation with decoration. The soul of Basque *nouvelle cuisine* is flavor. It is a discipline and a dedication to the selection and preparation of food in as uncomplicated a manner as possible, so as to release the inherent taste qualities. *Nouvelle* chefs work with the growers and purveyors to develop and locate ingredients with unmistakably superior flavor without regard to price, efficiency, or convenience.

The traditional, hearty Basque cuisine is filled with a great deal of dairy products from its lush pasturelands; fruits and vegetables from its fertile farms; good meat from the mountain meadows; and a wide variety of seafood from its cold Atlantic waters.

Everyone is a chef in the Basque Country. Fishermen create seafood miracles from a tradition of cooking on board as the catch is being made. It is the true meaning of the overworked supermarket term, "Catch of the Day." *Marmite*, the name of a spillproof cookpot designed for cooking aboard a boat, is a recipe usually made with fresh tuna, onion, garlic, and potatoes. Another favorite is salted cod simmered in a sauce of garlic, red peppers, onions, and bread crumbs that will make you change your ideas of what dried cod is supposed to taste like. The Basque seafood menu includes a long list of eel, anchovy, squid, tuna, shellfish, cod, hake, and mollusk. Some of the seafood cuisine is so sophisticated that it uses only small, select parts of the fish; in *kokotxas*, for example, small thin strips are cut from the "cheek" with a little olive oil, parsley, and garlic.

More than just the great quality and selection of the ingredients, Basque cooking relies on technique. The main feature is patient simmering, or *pil-pil*. It requires heating olive oil in an earthenware casserole (glazed on the inside surface and unglazed outside) to a temperature just below the boiling point before adding the ingredients. The dish is cooked very slowly and the pot is *shaken* from time to time, never stirred. The lid is never removed. The slow simmering allows the juices to bond with the olive oil to produce a thick, natural sauce. It is a simple, patient technique that produces a culinary distinction not found anywhere else.

The abundance of milk cow herds provides the Basque kitchen with sweet cream and butter, which appear frequently in basic Basque cooking. The region also produces excellent beef, lamb, and pork along with beautiful produce including corn, a great variety of beans, onions, potatoes, and garlic.

Obviously food is serious business in the Basque Country. Since 1900 the region has been the focus of an unusual form of social activity called *sociedades gastronómicas* — gastronomic societies. These organizations meet at night and were originally for men only. Some still are. The members select the recipes, purchase the ingredients, prepare the menu, serve it, enjoy it, and wash the dishes. The clubs maintain excellent wine cellars and the meetings are occasions of uproar and pleasure. Cooking contests are held among the members, sometimes among clubs. New recipes are created and new chefs are developed, many of whom go on to outstanding restaurant careers. There are over 1,000 gastronomic organizations in the Basque Country, a tremendous concentration of activity devoted to perfection of the culinary art. Rivaling Andalucía in its abundance of beautiful food, and Catalonia in its sophistication of preparation, the Basque Country is considered by many to be Spain's most interesting culinary center. There is no doubt that every Basque citizen will fight to preserve that honor.

THE WINES OF THE BASQUE COUNTRY

Almost all the wine of the region is produced in the southern area of the Basque Country adjacent to the Rioja. The Basque wines, called *chacolí* (*txakolí* in Basque), are young, fresh green wines and are very limited in quantity. They are pressed from two grapes: the white *Ondarrubi zuria* and the red *Ondarrubi beltza*. The wines are either white or rosé with low alcohol content and nice fragrance. They are excellent accompaniments to seafood dishes and are quite popular throughout the region.

Appetizers / Tapas

TOMATO AND PEPPER DRESSING WITH SHRIMP
ADEREZO DE TOMATES Y PIMIENTOS CON GAMBAS

Aderezo is typically Basque. It combines shrimp from the cold northern bay, spicy ingredients, and tasty vegetables. What's more, it is easy to prepare and will certainly make the party happen. Call it an original from the Sociedad Gastronómica.

SERVES 4

1   slice bread, crust removed, soaked in water and
      squeezed
1   clove garlic, peeled
2   tablespoons chopped onion
½   cup canned crushed tomatoes
3   tablespoons chopped green bell peppers
1   tablespoon chopped fresh cilantro
1   tablespoon sherry wine vinegar
½   teaspoon Tabasco sauce
    Salt to taste
½   cup olive oil
1   pound cooked jumbo shrimp, shelled

In a food processor or blender, mix all the ingredients except the olive oil and the shrimp. Blend until smooth. With the motor running, add the oil in a thin stream until smooth.

Pour the sauce into a serving bowl and dip the shrimp into it.

SARDINES AND PAPRIKA CANAPE
CANAPE DE SARDINAS CON PAPRIKA

This unusual combination of ingredients is another gift from the Basque culinary imagination. Sardines and heavy cream? Sherry wine vinegar and mayonnaise? Certainly not your usual canape, but it will surprise and delight you.

SERVES 8

1	can boneless sardines, drained
1	tablespoon mayonnaise
2	tablespoons heavy cream
2	tablespoons sherry wine vinegar
½	teaspoon paprika
	Freshly ground pepper
	Toast squares
6	pitted olives, sliced, for garnish

In a bowl mix all the ingredients except the toast and the olives. Blend well until smooth. Spread the mixture onto the toast and garnish with the sliced olives.

CHORIZOS AND PEARS IN HARD CIDER
CHORIZOS EN SIDRA

This is a tapa from my TV show. The flavors of the spicy sausage and the tangy hard cider are absorbed by the sweet, soft pears. Every bite is different. Ummm. Delicioso.

SERVES 4

1	tablespoon olive oil
6	chorizos, cut into about 5 pieces each
2	pears, peeled, seeded, and coarsely chopped
¾	cup hard cider
3	orange slices for garnish

In a large skillet, heat the oil and sauté the chorizos for about 3 minutes, shaking the pan briskly, until lightly golden. Add the pears and the cider and mix well. Cover and cook over medium-low heat for about 20 minutes or until the pears are slightly soft.

Remove mixture to a serving platter and garnish with the orange slices.

MUSSELS IN PARSLEY SAUCE
MEJILLONES EN SALSA VERDE

Believe me, you never ate anything so good. Sweet mussels simmered in their own juices and this wonderful salsa verde—it's enough to make a Basque warrior smile.

SERVES 4

4   cloves garlic, peeled
4   tablespoons chopped onion
¾   cup chopped flat parsley
¼   teaspoon dried oregano
¼   cup chicken broth
½   cup clam broth
3   tablespoons olive oil
2   tablespoons (1 oz.) dry sherry
1   tablespoon milk
1   teaspoon salt
¼   cup flour
2   dozen medium mussels, well scrubbed

In a food processor or blender, mix all the ingredients (a little at a time if necessary) except the mussels and blend well until smooth.

Pour the mixture into a large skillet, cover, and cook over low-medium heat for about 15 minutes, stirring until sauce thickens. Add the mussels and cook (covered) over medium heat, removing the mussels to a serving bowl as they open. Mix the sauce well and pour over the mussels.

Serve with hot French bread.

TUNA AND SHERRY CANAPE
CANAPE DE TUNA Y JEREZ

The mildness of the tuna and sherry is offset by the hot paprika or cayenne pepper. This canape does a lot of different things. The mild tuna and mellow Cheddar tease your taste. The sherry picks up the tempo, and the hot paprika or cayenne caps it off with a burst of Spanish spiciness.

SERVES 4 – 6

2	tablespoons (1 oz.) dry sherry
1	can (7 oz.) white tuna in water, drained
	Dash hot paprika or cayenne pepper
1	cup grated Cheddar cheese
	Freshly ground pepper
	Toast rounds

In a bowl, mix all the ingredients except the toast and blend well until smooth. Spread the mixture on the toast rounds and place them on an oiled or buttered cookie sheet. Bake in a 350° F preheated oven for about 5 minutes. Remove and serve.

Vegetables / Legumbres

POTATOES IN PARSLEY SAUCE
PATATAS EN SALSA VERDE

Potatoes are a Basque favorite. And potatoes in a salsa verde are incredible.

SERVES 4

1	cup chopped flat parsley
¾	cup clam broth or water
¾	cup chicken broth
¼	cup (2 oz.) dry sherry
¼	cup cream

    1   small onion, peeled and coarsely chopped
    7   cloves garlic, peeled
    2   tablespoons cornstarch
    ½   teaspoon oregano
    ½   teaspoon salt (or less)
    ¼   cup olive oil
    3   medium baking potatoes, blanched, peeled, and
           sliced into rounds
    2   tablespoons grated Parmesan

In a food processor or blender, mix all the ingredients except the potatoes and the cheese. Blend well until smooth.

Pour the mixture into a large deep skillet and heat over medium-high heat, stirring constantly until sauce thickens. Arrange the potato slices in the sauce. Cover and cook over low heat for about 10 minutes or until the potatoes are done.

Remove the potatoes and sauce to a serving platter and sprinkle with the Parmesan cheese.

ASSORTED VEGETABLES IN WHITE SAUCE
MENESTRA DE VEGETABLES EN SALSA BLANCA

Smooth, creamy, and sweet, this white sauce is one of my special touches from my restaurant. It will make vegetables taste wonderful. It will make rice sparkle. But it will make seafood get up and dance.

SERVES 4

    3   tablespoons olive oil
    1   bunch broccoli, trimmed and cut into florets
    1   medium zucchini, cut into 1-inch pieces
    1   medium yellow squash, cut into 1-inch pieces
    ¼   pound mushrooms, sliced
    1   green bell pepper, seeded and sliced
    2   tablespoons chopped parsley for garnish

WHITE SAUCE
    3   cloves garlic, peeled
    ¾   cup chopped onion
    ¼   cup melted butter (or less)

3	tablespoons olive oil
1/4	cup (2 oz.) dry sherry
1	bay leaf, crumbled
2	cups milk
1 1/2	teaspoons salt
1 1/2	tablespoons cornstarch

In a large deep skillet, heat the oil and sauté all the vegetables except the parsley, shaking the pan briskly and turning for about 5 minutes.

Meanwhile, in a food processor or blender, mix the ingredients for the white sauce and blend until smooth. Pour the sauce over the vegetables in the skillet and mix well until thickened. Cover and cook over low heat until vegetables are done.

Remove to a serving platter and garnish with the chopped parsley.

Salads / Ensaladas

DRIED COD FILLET SALAD
ENSALADA KOSHKERA

This salad is full of nutrition and is fat-free. Once the dried cod is soaked and drained, the rest is easy. Chop chop. Mix mix. It tastes so cool and delicious, your whole body will love it.

SERVES 4

1	pound salted dried cod, skinned and boned
1/2	cup virgin olive oil
3	cloves garlic, peeled and mashed
2	medium white potatoes, cooked, peeled, and cut into chunks
1	medium onion, peeled and thinly sliced
1/2	cup small stuffed Spanish green olives
1	canned pimento, whole, cut into strips
1/4	cup sherry wine vinegar
	Salt to taste
	Freshly ground pepper

Place the dried cod in a bowl and soak in water overnight. In a medium saucepan, bring 6 cups fresh water to a boil and cook the fish, covered, for about 20 minutes. Remove and let cool. When cool, shred the fish with a fork and set aside.

In a large salad bowl mix the oil, garlic, potatoes, onion, olives, pimento, vinegar, the shredded fish, and salt and pepper to taste. Mix well.

Refrigerate. Serve chilled on a bed of lettuce.

CUCUMBER SALAD
ENSALADA DE COHOMBRO

The Basque make something wonderful out of the simplest foods. Like a cucumber. Some spice. Some sweet. And you've got some dish.

SERVES 4

DRESSING
- 1   clove garlic, peeled
- ½   cup chopped onion
- 1   teaspoon honey
- ½   teaspoon salt
- ¼   teaspoon freshly ground pepper
- 6   tablespoons olive oil

- 8   cherry tomatoes, cut into halves
- 2   medium cucumbers, peeled and cut into rounds
- 1   large green bell pepper, seeded and coarsely chopped

In a food processor or blender, mix the dressing ingredients and blend until smooth. Reserve.

Place the tomatoes, cucumbers, and peppers in a salad bowl. Pour the dressing over the salad. Mix well and serve.

MIXED VEGETABLE SALAD WITH ANCHOVY DRESSING
ADEREZO DE ANCHOA CON ENSALADA

Crunchy bread . . . sangría . . . and some friends to go along with this unusual salad combination. It's another way the Basque apply their imagination to make every meal a taste experience.

SERVES 4

2   large tomatoes, cored and cut into chunks
2   medium cucumbers, peeled and sliced
1   small onion, peeled and sliced

DRESSING
2   cloves garlic, peeled
2   tablespoons chopped fresh cilantro
4   small stuffed olives
¼   teaspoon oregano
6   anchovy fillets
2   tablespoons seasoned bread crumbs
3   tablespoons red wine vinegar
¾   cup olive oil
    Salt to taste
    Freshly ground pepper

In a mixing bowl, combine the tomatoes, cucumbers, and onion. Set aside.

In a food processor or blender, mix all the ingredients for the dressing and blend until smooth. Pour the dressing over the vegetables and mix well. Refrigerate for about 1 hour and serve chilled.

Soups / Sopas

CABBAGE AND BEAN SOUP
SOPA DE BERZA Y HABAS (ELTZEKARIA)

This soup is typical of Basque Country cooking. It is simmered slowly, with plenty of flavor and high nutrition. So take your time and get the feeling of a tiny stone cottage tucked into a deep forest on a mountainside.

SERVES 4

1	medium cabbage, cleaned and cut into quarters
1	medium onion, peeled and chopped
3	cloves garlic, peeled
3	tablespoons chopped flat parsley
1	cup chicken broth
½	cup melted butter
16	ounces white navy beans, soaked overnight and drained
¼	cup (2 oz.) dry white wine
5	cups water
1	teaspoon paprika
	Salt to taste
	Freshly ground pepper
4	sprigs parsley for garnish

In a large saucepan, bring 6 cups water to a boil and cook the cabbage until tender. Drain and set aside.

In a food processor or blender (a little at a time if necessary), mix the onion, garlic, flat parsley, the reserved cabbage, broth, and butter. Blend well until smooth.

In a large casserole, combine the blender mixture, the beans, wine, 5 cups water, paprika, and salt and pepper to taste. Mix well, cover, and cook over low heat for about 2 hours or until the beans are done.

Serve in individual bowls and garnish with the parsley sprigs.

GARLIC SOUP BILBAO STYLE
SOPA DE AJO ESTILO BILBAO

I have a friend in Bilbao, Pedro Perea, who gave me this recipe. "I hope you like garlic," he said. I hope you like garlic, too.

SERVES 4

7	cloves garlic, peeled
1	teaspoon paprika
2	tablespoons chopped flat parsley
2	cups chicken broth
1	tablespoon cornstarch
¼	cup olive oil
4	cups hot water
1	tablespoon salt
	Freshly ground pepper
4	eggs, lightly beaten, or egg substitute equivalent
4	thick slices French bread
2	tablespoons chopped parsley for garnish

In a food processor or blender, mix the garlic, paprika, flat parsley, broth, cornstarch, and olive oil. Blend until smooth.

In a large casserole, pour the blender mixture and add the water and salt and pepper to taste. Cook uncovered over medium heat, stirring until soup starts to thicken. Reduce the heat to low and continue cooking uncovered for about 30 minutes. Add the beaten eggs very slowly while stirring.

Serve in individual soup bowls and garnish with the slices of bread and a sprinkle of chopped parsley.

FISH AND TOMATO SOUP
SOPA DE PESCADO Y TOMATE

I got this recipe from the Parador de Argomaniz in the Basque mountains. I added the carrots and cilantro for a little more crunch and a little more bite.

SERVES 4

3	tablespoons olive oil
4	cloves garlic, peeled and mashed
1	cup chopped onion
2	tablespoons chopped fresh cilantro
2	cups canned crushed tomatoes
½	cup (4 oz.) dry white wine
1¾	cups fish broth
½	pound salmon fillets, skinned, cut into chunks and lightly salted
½	pound scrod fillets, skinned, cut into chunks and lightly salted
¼	teaspoon cayenne pepper
2	carrots, peeled and cut into 1-inch rounds
	Salt to taste
	Freshly ground black pepper
4	lemon slices for garnish

In a large casserole, heat the oil and sauté the garlic, onion, and cilantro until onion is soft. Add the tomatoes, wine, broth, salmon, scrod, cayenne pepper, carrots, salt and black pepper to taste. Bring to a boil. Mix well, cover, and cook over low heat for about 45 minutes or until the carrots are tender.

Serve in individual soup bowls and garnish with lemon slices.

Rice / Arrozes

SEAFOOD PAELLA
PAELLA DE MARISCOS

Although the traditional Spanish influence is seen in the Basque paella, it is almost always made with a great seafood variety instead of meat and fowl. Well, I already told you the Basque are muy diferente.

SERVES 6 – 8

½	cup olive oil
4	lobster tails, split lengthwise
16	jumbo shrimp in their shells
5	cloves garlic, peeled and mashed
1	large onion, peeled and chopped
3	tablespoons chopped fresh cilantro
1	large tomato, seeded and chopped
2½	cups water
3	cups fish broth
½	cup (4 oz.) dry white wine
½	teaspoon crumbled saffron
2	bay leaves
1	canned whole pimento, chopped
½	teaspoon paprika
4	canned anchovy fillets, chopped
1	tablespoon salt (or less)
3	cups uncooked short-grain rice
¾	cup frozen peas
½	pound swordfish steaks, cut into chunks
½	pound scrod fillets, cut into chunks
	Butter
6	small clams, scrubbed well
6	medium mussels, scrubbed well
2	tablespoons chopped parsley for garnish
6	orange slices for garnish

In a large paella pan, heat the oil and sauté the lobster and shrimp until they turn pink. Remove to a warm platter and set aside. In the same pan, sauté the garlic, onion, and cilantro until the onion is soft. Add the tomato, water, broth, wine, saffron, bay leaves, pimento, paprika, anchovies, and salt to taste. Bring to a boil. Add the rice and peas and mix well.

Cook over medium-high heat until rice is semi-dry but some liquid remains. Bury the reserved shrimp and the fish chunks in the rice. Arrange the reserved lobster in the middle of the pan and dot with butter. Place the mussels and clams around the lobster, with the hinges facing down. Bake in a 325° F preheated oven for about 15–20 minutes or until the rice is dry and the shellfish have opened. Discard bay leaves.

Remove pan to a heat-resistant countertop and garnish with the chopped parsley and the orange slices.

WHITE RICE WITH DRIED COD
ARROZ BLANCO CON BACALAO

In the Basque Country cod is god.

SERVES 4

¼   cup olive oil
4   cloves garlic, peeled and mashed
½   pound salted dried cod fillet, soaked in water
       overnight, drained and shredded
4   cups chicken broth
2   cups uncooked short-grain rice
     Salt to taste
2   tablespoons chopped parsley for garnish

In a large casserole, heat the oil and sauté the garlic and the shredded cod for about 2 minutes. Mix well. Add the broth and bring to a boil. Add the rice and salt to taste and continue cooking, uncovered, for about 10 minutes or until the rice is semi-dry but some liquid remains.

Cover and cook over low heat for about 20 minutes or until the rice is dry. Turn the rice over with a fork from bottom to top and continue cooking, covered, for about 5 minutes more.

Remove the rice to a serving platter and garnish with the chopped parsley.

Serve this dish with Mussels in Parsley Sauce.

Shellfish / Mariscos

SHELLFISH WITH WALNUTS AND MUSHROOMS
MARISCOS CON NUECES Y SETAS

This dish has 15 ingredients. A lot? Not really. Ten minutes here, 10 minutes there, and you have a fabulous seafood meal that will excite you.

SERVES 4

5	tablespoons olive oil
½	pound large shrimp, shelled
½	pound sea scallops
4	cloves garlic, peeled and mashed
1	medium onion, peeled and chopped
2	tablespoons chopped flat parsley
1½	cups canned crushed tomatoes
½	cup clam broth
1	bay leaf
½	cup (4 oz.) dry white wine
½	cup ground walnuts
¼	cup (2 oz.) brandy
	Salt to taste
	Freshly ground pepper
1	cup small mushrooms (caps only)
3	orange slices for garnish
3	sprigs parsley for garnish

In a large skillet, heat the oil and sauté the shrimp and scallops briefly until shrimp is halfway cooked, about 3 minutes. Remove the shrimp and scallops to a warm plate and set aside.

In the same skillet, sauté the garlic, onion, and flat parsley until onion is soft. Add the tomatoes, broth, bay leaf, wine, walnuts, brandy, and salt and pepper to taste. Mix well. Cook uncovered over medium-low heat for about 10 minutes, stirring occasionally. Add the reserved shrimp, scallops, and the mushrooms and mix well with the sauce. Cover and cook over low heat for about 10 minutes more or until the shellfish is tender. Discard bay leaf.

Remove to a serving platter and garnish with the orange slices and parsley sprigs.

A great accompaniment to this shellfish dish is Potato Salad Valencia Style.

LOBSTER IN SEAFOOD SAUCE
LANGOSTA A LA VASCA

My friend Pedro Perea got this recipe from his Sociedad Gastronómica. They probably drank plenty of wine and they made sure some of it went into the sauce.

SERVES 4

¼	cup butter
4	lobster tails, split lengthwise
½	pound shrimp, shelled, cooked
3	cloves garlic, peeled
1	small onion, peeled and chopped
1½	cups canned crushed tomatoes
½	cup (4 oz.) dry white wine
¼	teaspoon crushed red pepper
¼	cup milk
	Salt to taste
	Freshly ground pepper
3	tablespoons olive oil
4	lemon slices for garnish
4	sprigs parsley for garnish

In a large skillet, heat the butter and sauté the lobster until lobster turns pink. Remove and set aside.

In a food processor or blender (a little at a time if necessary), mix the rest of the ingredients except the garnish and blend until smooth.

Pour the sauce into the skillet and bring to a boil. Cover and cook over low heat for about 10 minutes. Return the lobster to the skillet and continue cooking, uncovered, until lobster is tender.

Remove the lobster to a serving platter and pour the sauce over it. Garnish with the lemon slices and parsley sprigs.

This dish goes well with curly pasta.

Fish / Pescado

FISH AND CLAMS IN PARSLEY SAUCE
MERLUZA A LA VASCA (SALSA VERDE)

The star of this recipe is Doña Plácida de Larrea of Bilbao. In 1723 she wrote a letter to a friend in Navarra describing her delight with this meal. She specified that "the fish must be caught from a small boat by hook and line" and further described how the fish was stewed with shellfish and a green sauce made from parsley. Two hundred seventy years later we are still enjoying this wonderful salsa verde recipe. I, of course, could not leave history alone and have added my own touches to the recipe, dry sherry and oregano. Call it Salsa Verde a la Chef Ef.

SERVES 4

SALSA VERDE
  5 cloves garlic, peeled
  5 tablespoons chopped onion
 ¾ cup chopped flat parsley
 ½ teaspoon dried oregano
 ½ cup chicken broth
 ½ cup clam broth
 ¼ cup olive oil
  3 tablespoons dry sherry
  2 tablespoons milk (optional)
  1 teaspoon salt (or less)
 ¼ teaspoon freshly ground pepper
  5 tablespoons flour

  4 hake or cod fillets (about 8 oz. each)
 16 small clams, scrubbed
  2 tablespoons chopped pimento for garnish
  3 lemon slices for garnish

In a food processor or blender, mix all the salsa ingredients (a little at a time if necessary). Blend until smooth and reserve.

Sprinkle the fish with salt and pepper and place it in a baking dish. Pour the reserved mixture over the fish and bury the clams in the sauce with hinges facing down. Bake in a 350° F preheated oven for about 30 minutes or until the fish is done and the clams are open.

Remove the fish to a serving platter and arrange the clams around the fish. Mix the sauce well and pour over the fish and clams. Garnish with the chopped pimento and the lemon slices.

Serve with hot and crunchy bread for dipping.

SCROD IN CUCUMBER AND ROSEMARY SAUCE
PESCADO CON SALSA DE ROMERO Y COHOMBRO

The Basque are known for their sauces. Long, slow simmering without stirring is known as pil-pil *and creates a very deeply flavored sauce that is naturally thick and smooth. Once you make the sauce it can be used for vegetables, fish, meat, or salad. So make plenty. Freeze some. After all, who has time for* pil-pil *every day?*

SERVES 4

4	scrod fillets (about 6 oz. each)
	Salt to taste
	Freshly ground pepper
	Flour for dusting
3	tablespoons butter
1	tablespoon olive oil
2	tablespoons chopped parsley for garnish
4	orange slices for garnish

SAUCE

2	cloves garlic, peeled
4	tablespoons chopped onion
1	medium cucumber, peeled and cut into pieces
1	cup clam broth or fish broth
1	teaspoon dried rosemary
½	teaspoon salt
2	tablespoons chopped flat parsley
¼	cup heavy cream
1	tablespoon dry sherry
1½	tablespoons cornstarch
½	cup olive oil

Sprinkle the fish with salt and pepper and dust with flour.

In a large skillet, heat the butter and oil and sauté the fish on both sides until done. Remove the fish to a serving platter and keep warm.

In a food processor or blender, mix all the ingredients for the sauce and blend well until smooth. Pour the sauce into the skillet and cook uncovered over high heat, mixing with a whisk, until sauce thickens.

Pour the sauce over the fish and garnish with the chopped parsley and the orange slices.

Serve this recipe with baked potatoes and mixed vegetables.

BROILED SOLE WITH BASIL
LENGUADO ESTILO BERMEO

I tried this dish at the Centro Vasco Restaurant in New York City. I added the red wine vinegar for a little more spark. You could use balsamic vinegar just as well. Either way, this dish is especially fragrant and delicious. My compliments to the Centro Vasco.

SERVES 4

4	sole fillets (6–8 oz. each)
	Salt to taste
	Freshly ground pepper
¼	cup olive oil (for sautéing)
5	cloves garlic, peeled
1	tablespoon red wine vinegar
8	large sweet basil leaves
¾	cup virgin olive oil (for basting mixture)
2	tablespoons chopped parsley for garnish
4	lemon slices for garnish

Sprinkle the fish with salt and pepper, brush with the ¼ cup olive oil, and place in a broiler pan.

In a food processor or blender, mix the garlic, vinegar, salt to taste, basil, and the ¾ cup olive oil. Blend until smooth. Pour the mixture into a small bowl and set aside.

Place the fish under the broiler with low heat or on a low shelf and brush with the blender mixture several times until done.

Remove to a serving platter and sprinkle with the parsley and garnish with the lemon slices.

Serve with Saffron Rice.

DRIED CODFISH WITH POTATOES
BACALAO A LA VIZCAINA

My grandmother used to make this dish. She always made a lot of it for three good reasons: one, we were a large family; two, it was a great leftover served cold or even more delicious when reheated; and three, my grandfather liked it. So make plenty. Guess who's coming for dinner?

SERVES 4

1	pound salted dried cod fillets, skinned and boned
3	tablespoons olive oil
3	medium baking potatoes, peeled and cut into thin rounds
3	hard-boiled eggs, cut into rounds
2	medium onions, peeled and sliced
2	canned whole pimentos, sliced
¼	cup small stuffed olives
1	teaspoon capers
4	cloves garlic, peeled and mashed
2	bay leaves
½	cup raisins
¾	cup tomato sauce
¾	cup olive oil
	Salt to taste

Place the cod in a bowl of water and soak overnight, changing the water a few times. Drain. Shred the fish with a fork and set aside.

Coat the bottom of a large casserole with 3 tablespoons olive oil. Arrange the potatoes in layers to cover the bottom of the casserole. Spread the shredded cod on top of the potatoes. Arrange the egg slices, onion, pimento, olives, capers, garlic, bay leaves, and raisins over the fish. Add the tomato sauce and ¾ cup oil and bring to a boil. Cover and cook over low heat for about 30 minutes. Add salt to taste and turn with a fork from bottom to top. Discard bay leaves. Serve hot or cold.

I have tried many side dishes with this recipe, but have finally decided it is best served simply with white rice.

Meat / Carnes

VEAL IN TARRAGON SAUCE
TERNERA A LA TARRAGÓN

I was inspired by some of the veal recipes found on the menus of some Basque restaurants. Typical veal dishes are limited to veal piccata, scallopini, or parmigiana. This recipe creates a deep, interesting herbal flavor combined with the tender, sweet veal. The Basques know how to create flavor.

SERVES 4

1½	pounds veal cutlets, trimmed and pounded
	Salt to taste
	Freshly ground pepper
3	tablespoons butter
3	tablespoons olive oil
3	cloves garlic, peeled and mashed
1	medium onion, peeled and finely chopped
1	teaspoon dried tarragon
1¾	cups milk
¼	cup (2 oz.) dry white wine
3	tablespoons flour
1	tablespoon chopped parsley for garnish

Sprinkle the veal with salt and pepper and rub it into the meat.

In a large skillet, heat the butter and oil and sauté the veal briefly on both sides. Remove to a warm platter.

In the same skillet, sauté the garlic, onion, and tarragon until onion is soft. Add the milk, wine, salt to taste, and the flour. Cook over medium heat, stirring frequently until sauce is thickened. Return the veal to the skillet, cover, and cook over low heat until the veal is tender, about 15 minutes.

Remove the veal and the sauce to a serving platter and garnish with the chopped parsley.

Serve this dish with Escarole with Olives and Cheese.

Desserts / Postres

VANILLA CUSTARD
NATILLA

Keep it light and make it easy. And please your palate with this traditional custard. Maybe even have a cookie or two, too.

SERVES 4

1¾   cups milk
1   tablespoon cornstarch, dissolved in 3 tablespoons
      water
   Dash of salt
½   cup fine sugar
1   cinnamon stick
½   teaspoon vanilla extract
2   egg yolks, lightly beaten

In a large saucepan, combine the milk, dissolved cornstarch, salt, sugar, cinnamon, vanilla, and egg yolk. Mix well until smooth. Cook uncovered over medium heat and bring to a boil, stirring constantly, until thickened. Remove immediately and pour through a thin strainer into individual dessert cups. Refrigerate and serve chilled.

STEWED FIGS AND APRICOTS
ZURRACAPOTE

Watch these dried fruits come alive when you make this dish. A little wine and brandy adds to the pleasure of this beautiful fruit dessert.

SERVES 4

2   cups (16 oz.) red wine
¼   cup (2 oz.) brandy
1   cup sugar
1   teaspoon ground cinnamon
1   tablespoon lemon juice
½   pound dried pitted figs
½   pound dried apricots
   Fresh mint for garnish

In a large saucepan, combine the wine, brandy, sugar, cinnamon, and lemon juice. Bring to a boil over medium-high heat. Add the figs and apricots and mix well. Cover and cook over low heat for about 30 minutes. Remove to a large bowl and chill.

To serve, place several figs and several apricots in each of 4 small dessert bowls, pour some of the syrup over them, and garnish with fresh mint.

RICE PUDDING
PUDIN DE ARROZ

You have not tasted rice pudding until you try this classic version from my grandmother. It is thick and creamy with subtle flavors of brandy, sweet raisins, and cinnamon. It also makes a wonderful afternoon or late-night snack.

SERVES 10

6	cups milk
3¾	cups cooked white rice
6	teaspoons butter
5	eggs, beaten
2½	cups sugar
	Dash of salt
2	teaspoons vanilla extract
¼	cup (2 oz.) brandy
1½	cups raisins
	Cinnamon for dusting

In a large saucepan, heat the milk, rice, and butter over medium heat for about 5 minutes (do not overboil).

Meanwhile, in a small bowl, mix the eggs, sugar, and salt until smooth. Pour the egg mixture into the rice and mix well until thickened. Add the vanilla, brandy, and the raisins and mix well.

Transfer the rice mixture to a buttered baking pan and place pan inside a larger pan containing about 1 inch of water. Bake in a 350° F preheated oven for about 1 hour or until done.

Remove from the pan of water and let cool at room temperature.

Serve chilled in individual dessert bowls.

Pyrenees, San Juan de Plan

NAVARRA AND ARAGÓN

Navarra and Aragón are the unmarried sisters of Spain. Each was a kingdom of its own over a thousand years ago. Political and military conquests rearranged their borders, their alliances, and even their national homelands. Navarra was once a part of France and spelled itself *Navarre* for a period of history. It was also once a part of the Basque Country and once a part of Castile. In the eleventh century Aragón was united with Catalonia and controlled by the Counts of Barcelona. During this era Aragón became one of the most powerful maritime and trading nations of the Mediterranean. In the sixteenth century the territorial conflicts among Castile, the kings and counts of Aragón, Ferdinand, and France were finally settled and the present combined region of Navarra and Aragón became the quiet, northcentral place of peace and medieval memory.

Several examples of Moorish castles remain in Navarra and Aragón brooding over gray, stony sierras. Medieval castles, now hospitable paradors for the international visitor, are filled with the armor and chain mail worn in the great crusades and military campaigns of Charlemagne, Alfonso, and Ferdinand the Catholic. After the final union the great cathedral, Basilica de Pilar, was built on the banks of the River Ebro in Zaragoza. It was originally built as a small chapel to commemorate the miraculous appearance of the Virgin Mary in A.D. 40. The Catholic king, however, expanded the humble prayer house and it became the center of Spain's most important religious celebration, the Festival of El Pilar, which takes place in October.

Spain's most widely known festival, familiar throughout the world, is the running of the bulls in Pamplona, the capital of Navarra. It is also held during the religious holiday of St. Fermín. The city is

159

bedecked in red and white everything. The young men of the area, waving red cloths, join the rampaging herd of *toros* in a mad race of man and animal through the streets. Visitors come from all over the world, and the marathon excitement and merriment goes on day and night for a week. Café tables spill out into the streets and the great square is filled with music, dancing, wine, and feasting.

Between the holy processions and the madness of the bulls there is quiet. Trout abound in the sparkling streams of this northern province where Ernest Hemingway came to fish and rest as much as he came to experience the excitement of Pamplona. Like the Rioja country to the west, Navarra and Aragón are home to shepherds and their sheep, but it is mostly the quiet pursuit of a gentle life that occupies the people of this region.

Along the River Ebro is the fertile area of La Ribera. Fruit and vegetables are everywhere. The carefully tended orchards and small farms produce abundant crops of fruits that are among the best in Spain. Beautiful, sweet strawberries and apricots are harvested in late spring, followed by plums, cherries, peaches, and berries. The fall brings apples and pears with a special taste that comes from the clean, crisp autumn air and the well-irrigated land.

Many of the region's recipes are based on its wide variety of excellent produce. Garlic, onions, potatoes, and leeks are basic to the region's hearty stews and soups. Cabbage, lettuce, and cardoon (an edible thistle-like plant) are abundant, along with asparagus and artichokes. Tomatoes are plentiful, as are green peas and several varieties of beans. The region produces all kinds of sweet red peppers, including the very sweet pimento, all of which find their way into a great many recipes. The roasting of the peppers is a culinary tradition done in front of the houses over open fires. The peppers are basted with garlic, onion, salt, pepper, and olive oil; roasted; peeled and packed in jars for winter use; or sold to the tourists who are drawn to the peppery perfume that fills the air at roasting time. The red peppers are also strung to dry outside the village homes along with the chorizos. These quiet, colorful pursuits create the character of life in Navarra and Aragón.

In the northern portion of the regions along the border with France, near the Pyrenees, mushrooms are gathered. Quail, pigeons, and rabbit are hunted throughout the region, and the flocks of sheep provide a variety of famous lamb recipes. Pork is served often on the tables of Navarra and Aragón, in the form of pork belly, loin of pork, the ever-present chorizos, and hearty stews made with ham-bones.

The region produces good cheese made from ewe's milk. One strong variety is *queso de Roncal*, a hard, slightly greenish cheese, smoked and ripened for two months. Another is Idiazábal from the far north area. It is ripened in mountain caves and has a creamy texture with a delicate, smoky herbal taste.

Fresh fish, beautiful fruit and vegetables, along with wild game and home-raised meat contribute to hearty dishes for the people and visitors of Navarra and Aragón. The wine is less sophisticated than in many other regions of Spain, but Navarra and Aragón have a long tradition of winemaking from the third century B.C. The region produces high-alcohol–content wines with robust, strong character that reflects the personality and spirit of this part of Spain.

THE WINES OF NAVARRA AND ARAGÓN

NAVARRA

If politics and history had not interfered, the Navarra wine regions would have remained a part of the vinelands of the Rioja to the west. In fact, many wine firms of the Castilian Rioja buy their wine from the vineyards of Navarra.

Navarra grows the same grapes as the Rioja: the black Garnacha, Tempranillo, Graciano, and Mazuelo. Small amounts of the white Viura and Malvasía are also cultivated.

Although Navarra has been known for its red wines and especially its rosés being among the best in Spain since Roman times, the larger bodegas of Rioja bottle most of the wines produced in the Navarra region. Nevertheless, several small local bodegas bottle the wines and produce satisfying flavors that enhance the menus of Navarra.

ARAGÓN

The people of Aragón have been pressing the grape for over two thousand years. Ancient records indicate they drank a mixture of wine and honey three centuries before Christ. The land is not blessed with perfect climate; nevertheless, the region has managed to develop grape varieties that not only survive well but also produce wines of great strength and flavor. They are bottled and sold throughout Spain as a popular straight, high-alcohol wine that is loved at home but is unacceptable to foreign markets. As a result, most of the region's wine is sold for blending. It is in high demand for its strong character that heightens the flavor of lighter-tasting wines.

The grape that grows best in the difficult climate of Aragón is the black Garnacha. Some Garnacha blanca and Viura white grapes are grown as well, but in small amounts for local use. The Cariñena grape is also grown, producing a deep purple-colored wine with high alcohol content. It is full-bodied and deep in flavor, which becomes smoother and softer after oak-barrel aging. These are excellent wines and with some adjustments in the blending will receive wider acceptance.

Somontano wines are made from the black Garnacha and blended with other varieties. The result is a light wine with a low alcohol content and a fruity fragrance. Mostly sold in Spain, these wines received some popularity in France but remain a Spanish preference.

NAVARRA

Soups / Sopas

BEANS AND ASPARAGUS SOUP WITH HAM
SOPA DE HABAS Y ESPÁRRAGOS CON JAMÓN

The cold northern weather of Aragón/Navarra makes this a perfect soup for the hard-working mountain people. Although this hearty dish is delicious and satisfying, diet-conscious people will not prepare it regularly. But once in a while, why not?

SERVES 4

3	tablespoons olive oil
½	cup coarsely chopped onion
3	cloves garlic, peeled and mashed
3	tablespoons chopped fresh cilantro
2	chorizos, cut into 5 pieces each
¼	cup chopped salted pork (optional)
3	pork chops, boned and cut into pieces, or 1 hambone
½	cup (4 oz.) dry white wine
3	cups beef broth
2	cups water
4	small white potatoes, peeled and cubed
½	head of cabbage, shredded
2	10-oz. packages frozen limas
15	fresh asparagus spears, or 1 10-oz. package frozen asparagus, steamed and cut in half
	Salt to taste
4	sprigs parsley for garnish

In a large casserole, heat the olive oil and sauté the onion, garlic, and cilantro until onion is soft. Add the chorizos, salted pork, and pork chops and sauté for about 3 minutes. Add the wine, broth, water, potatoes, and cabbage. Bring to a boil. Cover and cook over low heat for about 1 hour or until the potatoes are soft. Add the beans, salt to taste, and continue cooking, uncovered, for about 20 minutes. Add the asparagus and cook for about 10 minutes more. Skim the foam from the top with a slotted spoon. Mix well.

Serve in individual soup bowls and garnish with a sprig of parsley.

Fish / Pescado

BAKED TROUT WITH HAM
TRUCHA ESTILO NAVARRA

Ernest Hemingway went to Aragón every year to chase the bulls in Pamplona and catch the trout in the mountain streams. So catch some trout, get the table ready, eat a beautiful classic meal, and raise a glass to Mr. Hemingway.

SERVES 4

4	trout fillets, (about 6–8 oz. each)
	Salt to taste
	Freshly ground pepper
	Lemon juice
½	cup fish broth
	Butter
½	teaspoon paprika
½	cup chopped serrano or prosciutto ham
8	lemon slices for garnish
2	tablespoons chopped parsley for garnish

Sprinkle the fillets with salt, pepper, and lemon juice and rub well.

Place the fillets in an oiled or buttered baking pan. Pour the fish broth along the sides of the fillets and dot with butter. Sprinkle the fillets with paprika and chopped ham and bake in a 350° F preheated oven for about 20 minutes or until the fillets are done.

Remove to a serving platter and garnish with lemon slices and chopped parsley.

Serve this dish with Asparagus in Saffron Sauce.

CODFISH IN GARLIC AND PEPPERS
BACALAO AL AJOARRIERO

This region of Spain is parador country—beautiful old castles, villas, and monasteries converted into modern hotels. This typical recipe comes from the Parador Nacional Principe de Viana in the area of Olite. You'll see how a simple piece of dried cod becomes a wonderful classic dish.

SERVES 4

1	pound salted dried cod fillets, skinned and boned
8	cups water
2	tablespoons olive oil
2	tablespoons butter (or less)
6	cloves garlic, peeled and mashed
1	medium onion, peeled and chopped
2	canned whole pimentos, drained and chopped
2	cups tomato sauce
2	tablespoons (1 oz.) brandy
1/4	teaspoon cayenne pepper
1	bay leaf
1	teaspoon capers
1	teaspoon salt (or less)
1/4	teaspoon freshly ground pepper
3	tablespoons chopped parsley for garnish

Soak the cod in a bowl of water overnight. Do not refrigerate. Change the water twice. Drain.

Place the cod in 8 cups boiling water and cook for about 10 minutes. Drain. Shred the cod with a fork and set aside.

In a large deep skillet, heat the olive oil and butter and sauté the garlic, onion, and pimentos for about 3 minutes or until onion is soft. Add the tomato sauce, brandy, cayenne, bay leaf, capers, salt, and pepper and mix well. Cook uncovered over medium heat for about 5 minutes, stirring the sauce well. Add the shredded cod and mix well. Cover and cook over low heat for about 20 minutes or until the cod is done. Discard bay leaf.

Remove the cod mixture to a serving platter and sprinkle with parsley.

Serve the cod with Broccoli, Walnuts, and Raisins.

Meat / Carnes

LAMB CHOPS WITH PEPPERS AND HONEY
CORDERO AL COCHIFRITO

The Navaronese love their lamb. They are the Little Bo Peeps of Spain. This cochifrito (stew) is one of the traditional recipes of the region. My grandmother always made this dish with fresh tomatoes, cilantro, and pimentos. The honey was my idea. Maybe you have your own ideas— like mint jelly or maple syrup.

SERVES 4

8 loin lamb chops (4 oz. each), trimmed
5 tablespoons olive oil (or less)
¼ cup (2 oz.) dry white wine
½ cup honey, mixed well with ¼ cup hot water
2 cloves garlic, peeled and mashed
½ cup chopped onions
1 tablespoon chopped fresh cilantro
1 cup canned whole tomatoes, drained and chopped
2 canned whole pimentos, coarsely chopped
   Salt to taste
   Freshly ground pepper
4 sprigs parsley for garnish

In a large skillet, heat 2 tablespoons olive oil and sauté the chops for about 20 minutes, turning them several times while cooking. Add the wine and shake the pan briskly until most of the liquid is evaporated and the chops are done. Arrange the chops on a serving platter and brush with the honey mixture. (Keep the chops warm.)

Wipe off the skillet, heat the remaining oil, and sauté the garlic, onion, and cilantro until onion is soft. Add the tomatoes, pimentos, salt, and pepper to taste. Mix well. Cook over medium heat uncovered for about 10 minutes, stirring the sauce occasionally.

Pour the sauce over the chops and garnish with parsley sprigs.

This dish goes very well with Chick-peas and Potatoes.

Desserts / Postres

ALMOND AND WALNUT CUSTARD
FLAN DE ALMENDRAS

This recipe will get you plenty of applause, lots of ooohs and ahhhs, and a few ummms. The contrast between the smooth custard texture and the crunchy nuts makes you want to eat all there is and more.

SERVES 8

1	cup sugar for caramelization
1	tablespoon water
4	ounces almonds, peeled and ground, or ½ cup
1	teaspoon grated lemon peel
6	eggs
1	cup sugar
¼	teaspoon salt
3	cups milk
½	cup chopped walnuts for garnish

In an 8-inch x 3-inch baking pan (8-inch round pan, 3 inches deep), caramelize 1 cup sugar and 1 tablespoon water until a light golden color. Cover the bottom and sides of the pan with the caramelized sugar and let cool.

In a food processor or blender, mix the rest of the ingredients (except walnuts) until smooth. Strain the mixture from the blender into the cara-melized pan. Place the pan inside a larger pan that has been filled with one inch of water. Bake in a 350° F preheated oven for about 1 hour or until a golden color. Remove the custard pan from the pan of water and let cool. Place the pan of custard in the refrigerator. When chilled, flip the custard onto a serving platter and garnish with the chopped walnuts.

Serve with dark coffee and lemon peel.

APPLE PRESERVES
PRESERVA DE MANZANAS

An apple a day keeps the doctor away. But if you serve apples like this, the doctor will come over; so will the butcher, the baker, and the candlestick maker, along with all of your amigos. So make mucho of this Spanish applesauce.

SERVES 4–6

6   tablespoons sugar
1   cup water
2   tablespoons (1 oz.) brandy
1   cinnamon stick
6   tart apples, cored, cut into eighths
    Whipped cream

In a medium saucepan, combine the sugar, water, brandy, and cinnamon stick. Cook over low heat for about 5 minutes. Add the apples, mix well, and cook uncovered over low heat for about 10 to 15 minutes or until the apples are tender.

Remove the apples to a serving bowl and continue cooking the syrup until it is a smooth consistency, stirring occasionally. Discard the cinnamon stick. Pour the syrup over the apples and serve chilled.

Whip up some whipped cream and serve in a separate bowl. Let everyone do themselves in.

ARAGÓN

Salads / Ensaladas

TOMATOES WITH RONCAL CHEESE
ENSALADA DE QUESO RONCAL

The region of Aragón/Navarra grows some of the finest vegetables in all of Spain. Maybe that's why they also have so many rabbits running around wild. Rabbits, however, don't eat tomatoes, so the people use plenty of tomatoes in many of the region's recipes. There are also plenty of goats and sheep that produce plenty of milk for two different strong, low-fat cheeses (Idiazábal and Roncal). So from the tomatoes and the cheese you get to eat this fabulous salad that will please your palate and protect you from el gordo.

SERVES 4

½ cup low-fat yogurt
1 small egg yolk or 2 slices of bread, crust removed
1 teaspoon lemon juice
1 cup Roncal cheese or domestic goat cheese at room temperature or softened
1 scallion, green part only, chopped
½ cup olive oil
4 medium ripe tomatoes, cut into halves, scooped out to form shells
4 medium lettuce leaves for garnish
1 tablespoon finely chopped scallion, green part only, for garnish

In a food processor or blender, add the yogurt, egg yolk or bread, lemon juice, cheese, and scallion. Blend well. With the motor running, add the olive oil in a thin stream until mixture is smooth.

Place the tomatoes on top of the lettuce in individual salad plates. Fill them with the cheese mixture.

Garnish with chopped scallions and serve at room temperature.

Shellfish / Mariscos

LOBSTER IN PEPPER STEW
LANGOSTA A LA ARAGÓN

There is a parador in the mountains of Aragón called Monte Perdido where you can swim, hike, climb to the top of the mountain and see the world, play tennis, and eat this wonderful lobster stew. What more could you want? Maybe más langosta, por favor.

SERVES 4

4   medium lobster tails, split lengthwise
¼   cup butter (or less)
5   cloves garlic, peeled
1   small onion, peeled and chopped
1   large green bell pepper, seeded and chopped
1   canned whole pimento, chopped
2   tablespoons chopped fresh cilantro
1   tablespoon paprika
1   tablespoon sherry wine
1   cup clam broth
1   teaspoon salt (or less)
1   tablespoon cornstarch
¼   teaspoon freshly ground pepper
¼   cup olive oil
4   lemon slices for garnish
3   sprigs parsley for garnish

In a large skillet, heat the butter over medium heat and sauté the lobster until it just turns pink. Remove and set aside.

In a food processor or blender, mix the rest of the ingredients except the garnish and blend until smooth.

Pour the mixture into the skillet and bring to a boil. Cook uncovered over low heat for about 5 minutes, stirring the sauce frequently until it thickens.

Return the lobster to the sauce, cover, and continue cooking for about 10 minutes or until lobster is done.

Remove the lobster to a serving platter and pour the sauce over it. Garnish with lemon slices and parsley sprigs.

Serve this dish with one of my Spanish rice dishes.

Poultry / Aves

CHICKEN WITH RED PEPPERS
POLLO CHILINDRÓN

This is one of the most typical dishes of Aragón. Everywhere you go you will find this dish. I have made some changes to make it easier for us busy people. I love it and I know you will love it, too.

SERVES 4

2½   pounds chicken, cut into serving pieces
      Salt to taste
      Freshly ground pepper
¼   cup olive oil
3   cloves garlic, mashed
1   large onion, coarsely chopped
¼   cup chopped chorizo
2   large red bell peppers, seeded and coarsely chopped
1   large tomato, chopped
2   tablespoons chopped parsley for garnish

Sprinkle the chicken with salt and pepper, rub it in well, and set aside.

In a large skillet, heat the oil and sauté the chicken until the skin begins to crisp all over. Remove to a warm platter and set aside.

In the same oil, sauté the garlic, onion, and chorizo until onion is soft. Return the chicken to the skillet and add the bell peppers, tomato, and pepper and mix well with the chicken. Cover and cook over low heat for about 35 minutes or until the chicken is tender. Remove the chicken to a serving platter. Stir the sauce for about 5 minutes and pour over the chicken. Garnish with chopped parsley.

This dish can be served with white rice and a green salad.

GARLIC CHICKEN
AJO BLANCO CON POLLO

Chicken is chicken until you make it with this recipe. The garlic is the taste that makes this chicken dish really special and not the same old, same old, same old . . .

SERVES 4

2   pounds small chicken pieces
     Salt to taste
     Freshly ground pepper
1   teaspoon lemon juice
½   cup olive oil (or less)
6   cloves garlic, peeled and mashed
3   tablespoons fresh chopped parsley for garnish

Sprinkle the chicken pieces with salt, pepper, and lemon juice.

In a large skillet, heat the olive oil and sauté the chicken until golden. Remove and set aside.

In the same skillet, add the garlic and sauté until garlic starts to color. Return the chicken to the skillet and mix well with the garlic. Cover and cook over low heat for about 15 minutes or until chicken is done.

Remove the chicken and garlic mixture to a serving platter and sprinkle with the parsley.

I like to serve this dish with Potatoes and Greens, or try it with your favorite pasta.

Meat / Carnes

PORK IN WINE AND PEPPER SAUCE
CERDO CHILINDRÓN

Aragón is chilindrón *country. Peppers, peppers, peppers: red, green, hot, sweet, fresh, dried, crushed, and roasted.* Chilindrón *refers to the use of red peppers in cooking. Once you get used to cooking with sweet red peppers, maybe you'll even roast a few in the front yard and have dozens of strings out your bedroom windows just like the natives.*

SERVES 4

2   pounds pork, cut into strips
    Salt to taste
    Freshly ground pepper
3   tablespoons olive oil
3   orange slices for garnish
2   sprigs parsley for garnish

SAUCE
2   cloves garlic, peeled
2   medium red bell peppers, seeded and chopped
1   large onion, peeled and chopped
1   teaspoon paprika
½   cup (4 oz.) dry white wine
1   cup beef broth
1   teaspoon salt (or less)
1   tablespoon cornstarch
¼   cup melted butter

Sprinkle the pork with salt and pepper and rub it in well.

In a large skillet, heat the oil and sauté the meat until it starts to color. Remove and set aside.

In a food processor or blender, mix all the ingredients for the sauce and blend well until smooth. Transfer the mixture to the skillet and cook over medium heat (stirring while cooking) for about 5 minutes.

Return the meat to the mixture in the skillet. Mix well; cover and cook over low heat until the meat is tender. Check for seasonings.

Remove the meat to a serving platter. Mix the sauce well and pour it over the meat. Add the orange slices and the parsley sprigs as garnish.
Serve this dish with baked potato or a white rice dish.

Desserts / Postres

STRAWBERRY SHERBET
SORBETE DE FRESAS

If you have an ice cream maker you can create one of the best helados de fresas ever. On a hot summer day you can serve this dessert with strawberry or maple syrup. Then stand back.

SERVES 4 – 6

1	pound fresh strawberries, washed and hulled
1½	cups sugar
6	cups water
½	cup (4 oz.) brandy
½	cup orange juice
1	cup heavy cream

In a food processor or blender, mix all the ingredients except the cream and blend until smooth. Strain the mixture into a saucepan and bring to a boil until half of the mixture is evaporated. Pour the mixture into an ice cream freezer. Add the cream. Mix well and freeze.

PEACHES IN WINE
MELOCOTÓNES ARAGONÉSES

I prepared this recipe on my TV show. I turned my back for a minute and the production crew and staff licked the platter clean. Maybe it was the fresh ripe peaches. Maybe it was the great Rioja wine. Or maybe they were just plain hungry.

1	cup (8 oz.) dry red wine
¼	cup (2 oz.) Licor 43
¼	cup fine sugar
8	canned peaches, halved and drained, or ripe freestone peaches, blanched
½	cup chopped walnuts

In a medium saucepan combine the wine, liqueur, and sugar. Mix well. Cook uncovered over low heat, stirring occasionally, for about 15 minutes.

Place 2 peaches in each of 4 dessert bowls and pour the sauce over them. Garnish with the walnuts and serve chilled.

Montserrat (outside of Barcelona)

CATALONIA

Catalonia is Barcelona. It is Gerona, Lérida, and Tarragona as well — beautiful cities steeped in history as far back as the Egyptians. But it is Barcelona that is the heart and soul of Catalonia. Barcelona is the commercial center of Catalonia and all of Spain. It was here that the spice traders came from the Far East and helped establish Barcelona as the mercantile power of the Mediterranean. While the merchants of Catalonia were building the great fleets that dominated the Mediterranean and the western seas, the philosophers and educators were creating revolutionary social concepts. They defined a code of civil liberties, *Usatges*, which preceded the Magna Carta by almost a century. The working class was made aware of its human rights and its political influence. The ancient Catalán language was reestablished and is still in use today, proudly separate and apart from mainstream Spanish. Even today Barcelona maintains its own autonomous government, the *Generalitat*, which regulates the affairs of the city like a separate state. Barcelona is Spanish, but it remains proudly Catalonian. From its earliest power days in the twelfth century to its present cosmopolitan status as one of the great cities of the world, it has retained a unique identity: a city of kings and power; master of the Mediterranean; guardian of its people and patron to the scholar and the artist.

Among the crowded barrio of the city bounded by great avenues and plazas, one finds the ancient and the dramatic nouveau side by side. Roman and Moorish remains and medieval cathedrals share their historic places in Barcelona with strikingly futuristic art and architecture. Alongside dusty antique shops, small bars, and cafés, museums display the work of the most modern artists. Museums are filled with the work of Picasso, who broke the bounds of all form and line. Joan Miro's unique abstractions touch you with their mystery and feeling. The classic modernists like Goya haunt you with their dramatic paintings of history and human drama. And above it all and surrounding your vision is the work of Antonio Gaudí. His Pavillion in the Parque Guell is a wondrous architectural masterpiece of Gothic, Moorish, and Spanish influences and his own genius. Domes, towers, windows, walls, and undefined shapes are covered in patterns of ceramic tile. Each tiny piece was conceived and created by Gaudí's own mind and hand. All over Barcelona, Gaudí buildings leap out from between their classic Spanish neighbors with unique shapes and structures. Towering above all of this is the cathedral of La Sagrada Familia. Is it lace? Or stone? Is it sculpture? Or architecture? Is it a monument to the divine existence? Or an expression of artistic imagination free from all restrictions of space and matter? It is all of these—unfinished, unplanned, and unbelievably wondrous. It is beauty, power, and delicate design. And it is Barcelona.

In the center of Barcelona is the Ramblas, a broad, tree-lined avenue with a central promenade that leads to the port. Stalls line the walk selling items of every description—flowers, birds, antiques, books, art, souvenirs, and clothing. Open cafés beckon with *tapas*, wine, coffee, and hot chocolate. You are invited to sit and enjoy the passing parade of all the world. At the end of the Promenade, in the port plaza, stands a tall monument capped by a figure of Columbus pointing to the east. It represents the events of history past and the adventure of what lies ahead.

To the north of Barcelona is the resort area of Costa Brava. Classic Spanish seaside villages decorate the rocky coastline and sandy beaches. The beautiful Spanish coast brings sunseekers from all over the world. Just inland from the sophisticated resort villages lies the ancient city of Gerona. The city is built on the banks of the River Onar, and its flat-faced buildings cantilever over the water's edge. A huge Gothic cathedral with a Baroque tower dominates the city, a guardian of its beauty and tradition.

South of Barcelona on the coastline is Tarragona, filled with the remains of Roman architecture. It hosts a great cathedral with a huge rose window and one of the most remarkable collections of medieval sculpture and carvings. Tarragona produces wines for export from the city's port, which is directly linked to the *Avenida de las Bodegas*.

Catalonia is rich in Spanish history as far back as 500 B.C. with tremendous influences by the early Greeks and Romans. Catalonia, with its ports, mercantile power, intellectuals, and artists, is also the birthplace of classic Spanish cuisine. The first Spanish cookbook was the *Libre de Sent Sovi*, written in the Catalán language in the first half of the fourteenth century. It was followed in 1477 by the more extensive and elaborate *Libre de Coch* (*Book of Cookery*). Published in Barcelona and written by Maestre Ruperto de Nola, chef to Alfonso of Aragón-Catalonia, it contained 243 recipes of considerable variety and sophistication, instructions for the carving of meat and game, and the proper technique of table service. *Libre de Coch* was written in Catalan and then translated into Spanish by one of Europe's legendary gourmets, Charles V of Spain. It was eventually translated into many languages and was widely circulated beyond Spain.

The spectrum of Catalonian cooking is as varied as the many small localities, each of which prides itself on the specialized recipes that reflect its resources and culinary art. The Costa Brava area prepares seafood in endless variety. Mussels, monkfish, lobster, snails, crabs, and tiny clams are cooked with wine, almonds, peppers, saffron, mushrooms, onions, and garlic. *Zarzuela*, a Spanish word for musical variety show, is a mixture of shellfish and white fish cooked in a rich sauce of onions, garlic, and tomatoes. Lobster *(langosta)* is stewed with onions, carrots, garlic, herbs, chocolate, nutmeg, and brandy.

The inland areas are rich in meat and poultry dishes: baby goose or duck with pears; rabbit with tiny snails; oxtail with mushrooms; stuffed leg of lamb; quail stuffed with foie gras; pheasant with stewed apples, cloves, and nutmeg; and steak with Roquefort sauce. The Catalonian masters of cuisine invent, create, and present an endless variety of elegantly prepared main dishes that are memorable dining experiences. Vegetables are prepared with the same imagination and inventiveness: fresh young *habas*, a tiny lima-like bean, cooked no longer than three minutes, is an early season delight; young asparagus served with either warm or cold sauces; charred scallions; spinach cooked with garlic, anchovies, pine kernels, and raisins; creamed radishes; cucumber salad; mushrooms of every species; and sweet red peppers and pimentos.

Fresh and cooked fruits appear everywhere on the Catalonian

menu. Pears, peaches, figs, and apricots are cooked with meat and poultry. Every kind of melon is available in abundance and perfection. They are served with lemon, wine sauce, and ginger. Melon slices are wrapped in ham or salami and served with lime wedges. Melon salads are created with avocado or cheese and sweet orange sauce. Bowls of fresh fruit grace the dessert tables with enormous grapes, golden peaches, buttery pears, white and red cherries, tiny seedless oranges, and pale yellow plums with sugary flesh. Fruit became an art form in Spain; collectors prize the classic sixteenth- and seventeenth-century still-life paintings of sensual fruit and flowers bursting from their dark umber backgrounds.

Spices and herbs play their supporting roles in the culinary drama with tremendous impact. And no wonder. Barcelona was the port of spices, the motivation for the Columbian sea adventure that changed the world. Oregano, rosemary, thyme, and bay leaves are traditional and essential Catalonian herbs. Raisins, prunes, pine-nuts, honey, and ginger are Moorish touches present in the best Catalonian recipes.

With such bounty and focus on culinary creativity, the Catalonian chefs developed sauces that are basic to all the region's cooking. Of the many variations there are five essential sauces. The most basic is *Alioli*, a Roman original made by grinding garlic and olive oil with a mortar and pestle. *Picada* is a sauce mixture made with almonds and toasted hazelnuts. *Chanfaina* combines peppers, onions, tomatoes, and garlic for an all-purpose red salsa. *Chilindrón* is a spicier version of the *chanfaina* using hot, dried peppers. *Romesco* is a traditional sauce mostly used for fish dishes and made with hazelnuts or almonds, red peppers, garlic, onions, tomatoes, herbs, and a very good, fruity olive oil.

The historic traditions of Catalonian cooking place this region's recipes at the top of Spain's impressive list. Catalonian cuisine is recognized throughout the world as a standard of classic excellence. It is both sophisticated and primary; subtle and bold; delicate and robust. Meals are an experience to be slowly enjoyed and long remembered. The Catalonian chef begins with the mortar and pestle, and the diner ends the meal with a sigh of pleasure as the last taste of the fresh fruit sorbet and sparkling white *cava* linger on the palate.

THE WINES AND BRANDIES OF CATALONIA

The classic cuisine of Catalonia deserves, and is honored with, some of the finest wines of Spain. They are grown south of Barcelona along the coastal plains in an area called Penedés. Winemaking in the region began with the Greek, Phoenician, and Carthaginian settlers who lived along the Mediterranean coast around 500 B.C. It was the Romans, however, whose demand for wine was only exceeded by their need for conquest, who began planting vineyards on the palatial villas they built as part of the rights of conquerors. The dark post-Roman rule of the Visigoths and the temperate rule of the Arabs put the cultivation of vine and wine in decline. A revival took place after the reconquest and the establishment of great monasteries. Vineyards were planted and wineries built. As more and more land was reoccupied, feudal rental agreements were set up whereby tenant farmers shared their grape harvest with the landowners. Quantity was the goal and quality suffered.

The collapse of the French wine industry in the late 1800s due to diseased grapevines created an enormous demand for the Penedés wines. The boom busted, however, when the same disease crossed the border and devastated the Penedés vineyards. Replanting lasted until the Spanish Civil War took its greatest toll in the region of Catalonia and Penedés. It is only the last half century that has seen the south Catalonian wine industry rise again to new and greater heights. New varieties of grapes were sought out in Europe and America. Modern technology was introduced, and Catalonian wines have become among the best in Spain and highly desirable throughout the world.

The greatest single factor in the reemergence of Penedés wines was the production of sparkling wine. Originally modeled after French Champagne, the Spanish sparkling wines were called *champaña*, produced by the *methode champenoise*. A loud international complaint and an image as a less costly substitute led to the official denomination of *espumosos* and the more recent and popular term *cava*. *Cava* represents the pure Penedés process from grape to bottle, a designation of highest-quality sparkling wines in their own right with unique characteristics thanks to their place of origin and carefully chosen grape varieties.

The sparkling wines of Penedés are made from three native grape varieties: the white Macabeo, Xarel-lo, and Parellada. Freshness and fruit flavor are found in the Macabeo; character and high alcoholic content are derived from the Xarel-lo; and the Parellada adds a fine, gentle nose. The black Garnacha, a Spanish favorite, or the Cariñena are sometimes used to produce a delightful pink *cava*, while a touch of red Monastrel adds a fresh touch and promotes a longer life.

The two great *cava* producers of Spain are Cordorniu, one of Spain's oldest winemaking firms, and Freixenet, which has made a tremendous impact in the United States market with its very popular, low-priced "champagne." *Cava*, however, is not champagne. *Cava*, simply put, is considered among the best sparkling wines of the world, if not the finest.

The selection of a *cava* type is best made on the basis of individual preference. Cava is labeled from *extra dry* to *sweet*, with five degrees of sweetness in between. The Spanish taste prefers more sweetness; American and British tastes are more suited to a *Brut natur* (extra-dry) or *Brut* (dry). The *cava* process, which allows final fermentation to take place in individual bottles and is most like the original Champagne method, is clearly indicated on the cork stopper with a four-pointed star. Sparkling wines whose final fermentation takes place in pressurized tanks are marked with a circle. Sparkling wines created with a blast of carbon dioxide pumped under pressure into still wines are not marked—and not worth purchasing.

In addition to the *cavas*, the Penedés area of southern Catalonia produces a wide range of fruity red wines and refreshing whites. The Penedés area stretches along the Mediterranean coast and inland and upward to the interior mountains. The Baja Penedés, or lowlands, just in from the coast, is the warmest area and produces red grapes. Medio Penedés, the middle ground, produces about half of the Penedés white grapes; the cooler, higher Penedés Superior yields the delicate Parellada.

The best wines of Penedés are near the level of the Rioja wines, averaging four Very Good or Excellent vintage years out of every ten. In addition to the Penedés wine region there are seven other demarcated regions in Catalonia, each of which produces its own special wines affected by different climates and winemaking techniques.

Tarragona is the largest of the seven regions and produces strong red and white wines, mostly used for blending or everyday consumption. The area also produces a significant amount of sweet dessert wines, some containing as much as 23 percent alcohol. Tarragona is also home to the famous bodega of DeMuller, a maker of altar wine that it exports all over the world, especially to its prime client, the Vatican.

Priorato, west of Tarragona, lies in the land of scorching summer sun, and its black Garnacha and Cariñena grapes produce a delicious, full-tasting, rustic red wine with regional popularity.

West of the Penedés in the hills of Conca de Barbera, the clay soils are suited to several foreign grape varieties. Extensive plantings of Cabernet Sauvignon, Pinot Noir, and Chardonnay vines have begun. Much of the grape harvest is currently used in the making of *cava* and rosé regional wines.

Terra Alta, in the westernmost part of Catalonia, produces wines that are carefully and lightly hand-pressed. They are the *en virgen* wines, but nevertheless full-tasting and dry.

Alella, north of Barcelona, is the smallest wine region of Catalonia and suffers from urban blight. New restrictions on encroachment and building have preserved the small vineyards that produce rare white wines with a lovely fragrance and a light, refreshing taste.

Ampurdán-Costa Brava to the north cultivates vines on stakes to protect against the constant high winds. Nevertheless, this region produces excellent rosés; strong, high-fruit-flavor reds; and a Garnacha blanca white wine.

The area of Lérida has recently been renovated by the Cordorniu firm, and new techniques of irrigation, a modern bodega, and several outstanding varieties of grapes have begun to produce some of the best Catalonian wines. They include an excellent light Chardonnay; a nice dry white and a sweet white; a new, full rosé; and several excellent special blends that rival the taste and appeal of the most popular French wines. This is a remarkable accomplishment in a short period of time and can only contribute to the continued expansion of the fine Spanish wine list.

LIQUEURS AND BRANDY

Most Spanish brandy is made in Jerez de la Frontera, even though Catalonia has been at it longer. Fine wines are distilled in pot stills, the same technique used in the seventeenth century, and then aged in oak casks. The fine, powerful brandies are very similar to Cognac and preferred by many throughout Europe, especially in England. A Gran Licor de Naranja is also produced by steeping highly selected orange peel in alcohol and then distilling the mixture.

Tarragona produces the famous yellow and green Chartreuse liqueur that is made from a secret recipe of herbs known only to three men who produce the potion in an old distillery in Tarragona, as well as in another somewhere in the forests of France.

There is no doubt that the culture, cuisine, and wines of Catalonia combine to raise civilized pleasure to one of the highest levels in the world.

Appetizers / Tapas

COUNTRY BREAD WITH TOMATO AND HAM
PAN CON TOMATE Y JAMÓN

I made these tapas on the TV show. They are fast, easy, and muy
delicioso. *For your next Super Bowl party, it's a sure touchdown.*

SERVES 4

4	cloves garlic, peeled
¼	cup olive oil
½	teaspoon paprika
	Salt to taste
4	slices lightly toasted country-style bread
1	medium tomato, peeled and crushed
4	thin slices serrano or prosciutto ham

In a food processor or blender, combine the garlic, olive oil, paprika, and salt and blend until smooth.

Spread a thin layer of the garlic mixture over each slice of toasted bread, then spread 1 tablespoon of the crushed tomato on each slice. Top with a slice of ham.

Cut bread slices in half and serve.

GRILLED BEEF WITH GARLIC MAYONNAISE
CARNE CON ALIOLI

Alioli (garlic sauce) is the oldest sauce in Europe. It originated in ancient Rome by grinding garlic, olive oil, and salt with a mortar and pestle. I have created a modern version of this classic sauce with a little of this and a little of that and a mechanical blender instead of elbow grease. Warning: This sauce is for garlic lovers only.

SERVES 4

1½	pounds beef round steak, cut into 1-inch cubes
	Salt to taste
	Freshly ground pepper

ALIOLI SAUCE
1   egg yolk
6   cloves garlic, peeled
3   tablespoons chopped onion
½   teaspoon salt (or less)
1   teaspoon lemon juice
¾   cup olive oil

Sprinkle the meat with salt and pepper and arrange it in a broiler pan. Place the pan under a broiler and cook for about 10–15 minutes, turning once, or until meat is done. Remove to a serving platter and place a toothpick in each cube.

Meanwhile, in a food processor or blender, mix the egg yolk, garlic, onion, salt, and lemon juice and blend well. With the motor running, pour the olive oil in a thin stream until smooth. Transfer the blender mixture to a serving bowl. Present the platter of meat and the sauce for dipping.

CLAMS IN ROMESCO SAUCE
ALMEJAS EN SALSA ROMESCO

This is a very sophisticated sauce and a very flexible recipe. It's a great appetizer that makes a great meal over pasta, or it's a great meal served over pasta that makes a great appetizer.

SERVES 4

3   cloves garlic, peeled
½   cup chopped onion
1   tablespoon chopped fresh cilantro
¼   cup (2 oz.) dry white wine
¼   teaspoon cayenne pepper (or less)
¼   cup ground walnuts
¼   cup ground hazelnuts
1   cup clam broth
½   cup chicken broth
2   slices bread, crusts removed
1   tablespoon brandy
½   teaspoon dried rosemary
1   canned whole pimento, chopped

½   cup canned crushed tomatoes
¼   teaspoon freshly ground pepper
1   teaspoon salt (or less)
¼   cup olive oil
20 small clams, well scrubbed
3   tablespoons chopped parsley for garnish
3   lemon slices for garnish

In a food processor or blender, mix all the ingredients except the clams and the garnish, a little at a time if necessary. Blend well until smooth.

Transfer the mixture to a large skillet, mix well, and bring to a boil. Add the clams and cook covered over low heat until clams open. As they open, remove the clams to a serving platter. Continue cooking and stirring the sauce for about 3 minutes.

Pour the mixture over the clams. Garnish with chopped parsley and lemon slices.

SHRIMP IN GARLIC SAUCE
GAMBAS AL AJILLO

This dish was the biggest hit in my restaurant. People begged me for the recipe. And it's so simple. One pan, one minute—one great appetizer that could make you famous. Serve as an appetizer or as a main dish with one of my rice recipes or over pasta.

SERVES 4

½   cup olive oil
4   cloves garlic, peeled and mashed
1   pound large shrimp, peeled and deveined
½   teaspoon crushed red pepper
½   teaspoon salsa picante or Tabasco sauce
1   teaspoon paprika
3   tablespoons dry sherry
1   tablespoon tomato sauce
    Salt to taste
    Freshly ground pepper
1   tablespoon chopped parsley for garnish
4   lemon slices for garnish

In a large skillet, heat the oil and sauté the garlic and shrimp over medium-high heat for about 1 minute. Add the crushed red pepper, hot sauce, paprika, sherry, tomato sauce, and salt and pepper to taste. Mix well until shrimp is pink and done.

Remove to a serving platter. Sprinkle with parsley and garnish with lemon slices.

SOLE WITH RAISINS
LENGUADO CON PASAS

You can make this appetizer in one pan and one blender. Quickly sauté. Quickly blend. Pour and get out of the way. And be sure to make enough of this sweet and savory dish.

SERVES 4

1	pound sole fillets, cut into chunks
	Salt to taste
	Freshly ground pepper
	Flour for dusting
5	tablespoons olive oil
¼	cup chopped walnuts
½	cup white raisins
¾	cup boiling water
1	tablespoon honey
¼	teaspoon salt
1	teaspoon lemon juice
¼	cup melted butter (or less)
3	tablespoons chopped parsley for garnish

Sprinkle the fish with salt and pepper and dust with flour.

In a medium skillet, heat the oil and sauté the fish chunks until golden on both sides. Remove to a serving platter and keep warm.

In a food processor or blender, mix the walnuts, raisins, water, honey, salt, lemon juice, and butter. Blend until smooth.

Spoon some of the sauce over the fish chunks and sprinkle it with the chopped parsley.

OLIVES AND PINE NUTS CANAPE
TAPANADE DE ACEITUNAS Y PIÑONES

Whrrrrrrrrrrrrrrrrrrrrrrr. Spoon the mixture from the blender onto the toast and serve. It's that easy.

SERVES 4–6

2	cloves garlic, peeled
2	tablespoons chopped onion
1½	cups small Spanish olives, pitted, rinsed, and drained
1	teaspoon sherry wine vinegar
1	tablespoon pine nuts
2	tablespoons chopped fresh cilantro
¼	teaspoon freshly ground pepper
¼	cup olive oil
	Toast rounds

In a food processor or blender, mix all the ingredients except the toast rounds. Blend well until smooth. Spread a thick layer of the mixture onto the toast and serve.

SHRIMP IN SHERRY WINE
GAMBAS EBRIAS

Emilio's Tapas Bar Restaurant in Chicago creates hundreds of tapas. This is one of the best.

SERVES 4

¼	cup olive oil
2	cloves garlic, peeled and finely chopped
2	tablespoons chopped fresh cilantro
1	tablespoon paprika
½	cup dry sherry
	Salt to taste
1	pound jumbo shrimp, shelled
¼	cup raisins for garnish

In a medium skillet, heat the oil and sauté the garlic, cilantro, and paprika for about 1 minute. Add the sherry and salt and bring to a boil.

Add the shrimp, cover, and cook over low heat until shrimp is pink. Remove to a serving platter and garnish with raisins.

SHRIMP ALIOLI CANAPE
CANAPE DE GAMBAS EN ALIOLI

Every Spanish chef creates a unique version of Alioli. This one is mine. It's creamy, garlicky, and shrimpy.

MAKES 20 CANAPES

1	egg yolk
5	cloves garlic, peeled
3	tablespoons chopped onion
1	teaspoon lemon juice
¼	cup chopped cooked shrimp
½	teaspoon salt (or less)
1	cup olive oil
	Assorted crackers
2	tablespoons chopped parsley for garnish

In a food processor or blender, mix the egg yolk, garlic, onion, lemon juice, shrimp, and salt. Blend well until smooth. With the motor running, add the olive oil in a thin stream until smooth.

Place a small amount of the mixture over each cracker and sprinkle with chopped parsley.

Vegetables / Legumbres

BROCCOLI WITH WALNUTS AND RAISINS
BRÉCOL CON NUECES Y PASAS

Sweet, crunchy, spicy, and nutritionally powerful—these are just some of the benefits of this simple little dish. It is also muy delicioso.

SERVES 4

¼   cup olive oil
3   cloves garlic, peeled and mashed
½   cup chopped onion
¼   cup chopped walnuts
¼   cup raisins, blanched and drained
1   bunch broccoli, trimmed and cut into florets
¼   cup (2 oz.) dry white wine
     Salt to taste
     Freshly ground pepper

In a large skillet, heat the oil and sauté the garlic, onion, walnuts, and raisins until onion is soft. Add the broccoli, wine, and salt and pepper to taste. Mix well, cover, and cook over low heat for about 10 minutes or until the broccoli is tender. Remove to a serving platter.

CATALÁN STYLE SPINACH
ESPINACAS ESTILO CATALÁN

This spinach dish represents more than Popeye's muscles. It represents history. This classic Catalán recipe will change all your ideas about spinach and add a wonderful vegetable dish to your family table.

SERVES 4

¼   cup olive oil
2   cloves garlic, mashed
3   tablespoons chopped onion
6   anchovy fillets, chopped
4½   pounds spinach, washed, steamed, drained, and
        chopped
¼   cup pine nuts
¼   cup chopped raisins
     Salt to taste
     Freshly ground pepper
2   orange slices for garnish

In a large skillet, heat the oil and sauté the garlic, onion, anchovy, spinach, pine nuts, and raisins for about 5 minutes. Season with salt and pepper and mix well.

Transfer the mixture to a salad serving bowl and garnish with orange slices.

CHICK-PEAS AND POTATOES
GARBANZOS Y PATATAS

Here is the old-fashioned way my mother used to cook. Garbanzos y Patatas makes a perfect companion to many dishes. It is economical, palate pleasing, and filling. Call it family food.

SERVES 4

8	cups water
4	tablespoons olive oil
1	teaspoon salt
½	pound fresh chick-peas, soaked in water overnight
3	medium white potatoes, peeled
3	cloves garlic, peeled and mashed
1	medium onion, peeled and chopped
2	tablespoons chopped fresh cilantro
¼	cup chopped serrano or prosciutto ham
2	chorizos, cut into pieces
¼	cup (2 oz.) dry white wine
¾	cup canned crushed tomatoes
	Salt to taste
	Freshly ground pepper
3	sprigs parsley for garnish

In a large casserole, combine the water, 1 tablespoon of the oil, and 1 teaspoon salt. Bring to a boil. Add the chick-peas and cook over medium heat for about 30 minutes. Add the potatoes and cook 30 minutes more, or until the chick-peas are almost tender. Drain and set aside. Cut the potatoes in chunks and set aside with the peas.

In a large skillet, heat the remaining oil and sauté the garlic, onion, cilantro, ham, and chorizo until onion is soft. Add the wine, tomatoes, reserved chick-peas and potatoes, and salt and pepper to taste. Cover and cook over low heat for about 15 minutes or until the peas are tender.

Remove to a serving platter and garnish with parsley sprigs.

EGGPLANT WITH CHEESE
BERENJENA CON QUESO

This recipe of mine was inspired by Ruperto de Nola, author of Libre de Coch, *the historic Catalán cookbook published in 1477. The original recipe was created by King Alfonso, and now you can re-create it for your amigos y familia.*

SERVES 4

1½–2	pounds eggplant, peeled and cut into ½-inch slices
1	cup chicken broth
¼	cup ground walnuts
3	tablespoons chopped onion
1	tablespoon chopped flat parsley
	Salt to taste
	Freshly ground pepper
2	tablespoons olive oil
½	pound shredded mozzarella cheese
1	teaspoon ground cinnamon
1	teaspoon ginger
1	tablespoon chopped parsley for garnish

Place the eggplant slices in a baking pan with ¼ cup of the broth. Bake in a 375°F preheated oven for about 10 minutes or until almost cooked.

Meanwhile, in a food processor or blender, mix the walnuts, onion, flat parsley, the remaining broth, salt and pepper to taste, and the oil. Blend until smooth. Pour the mixture over the eggplant. Cover each slice with cheese and sprinkle cinnamon and a dash of ginger over the cheese. Continue baking for 10 minutes more or until the cheese has melted.

Remove the eggplant to a serving platter. Pour the sauce over it and garnish with chopped parsley.

Salads / Ensaladas

CODFISH AND WHITE BEAN SALAD
ENSALADA A LA CATALANA

Historically, the Spanish people have always had dried cod recipes to fall back on during hard times. The recipes are delicious, hearty, and can be flavored and spiced many ways. Dried cod is always available, inexpensive, and, once cooked, it keeps for weeks. You can cook it once, but you can eat it again and again and again. And love it every time.

SERVES 4–6

1	pound salted dried cod fillets, skinned and boned
1	small onion, peeled and sliced
12	ounces (1½ cups) cooked small white beans, drained
½	cup small stuffed green olives, rinsed and dried
2	tablespoons chopped fresh cilantro
1	large tomato, coarsely chopped
¼	cup red wine vinegar
¾	cup virgin olive oil
	Salt to taste
	Freshly ground pepper

Place the codfish in a bowl of water and soak overnight. Do not refrigerate. Drain. Boil codfish in 8 cups water for about 15 minutes. Drain again and shred with a fork.

Place the shredded fish in a large bowl and add the onion, beans, olives, cilantro, tomato, vinegar, olive oil, and salt and pepper to taste. Mix well. Refrigerate and serve chilled.

AVOCADO AND ORANGE SALAD
ENSALADA DE AGUACÁTE Y NARANJAS

The Old World and the New World come together in this salad. The Spanish explorers brought avocados back from South America and the groves of Spain produced the sweet orange fruit. Ahhh—what a beautiful marriage.

SERVES 4

2	avocados, halved lengthwise and seeded
1	8 oz. can mandarin oranges, drained and chopped
¼	cup raisins
¼	cup finely chopped walnuts
¼	cup olive oil
	Salt to taste
	Freshly ground pepper
4	sprigs parsley for garnish
	Lettuce

Scoop the meat out of each avocado without breaking the skin. Cut the avocado meat into small cubes and place in a bowl. Add the orange pieces, raisins, walnuts, olive oil, and salt and pepper to taste. Mix well. Spoon the mixture into the avocado shells and garnish with sprigs of parsley. Serve on a bed of lettuce.

Soups / Sopas

SHRIMP SOUP CATALÁN STYLE
SOPA DE GAMBAS A LA CATALANA

Ahhh. This is some soup. Beautiful vegetables, basil and garlic, chicken broth, and 16 large shrimp swimming around. Could you ask for more? You will when you taste it.

SERVES 4

3	tablespoons olive oil
3	cloves garlic, mashed
1	pound fresh spinach, trimmed and coarsely chopped
½	cup small stuffed green olives, rinsed
3	cups chicken broth
4	medium tomatoes, seeded and coarsely chopped
1	cup coarsely chopped fresh basil

Salt to taste
Freshly ground pepper
16   jumbo shrimp, shelled and deveined
2   tablespoons chopped parsley for garnish

In a large casserole, heat the oil and sauté the garlic, spinach, and olives until spinach begins to wilt. Add the broth, tomatoes, basil, and salt and pepper to taste. Mix well and bring to a boil. Add the shrimp and cook uncovered until the shrimp is cooked.

Serve in individual soup bowls and garnish with chopped parsley.

ESCAROLE SOUP
SOPA DE ESCAROLA A LA CATALANA

Escarole is often used in Spanish cooking. It is wonderful in soups, makes a great vegetable side dish, and creates a tangy, bittersweet salad that loves olive oil, black pepper, and lemon juice. Escarole is also very healthy. It provides excellent fiber and many vitamins. So . . . it's escarole tonight.

SERVES 4

1   cup water
1   pound escarole, trimmed and washed
2   cloves garlic, peeled
¼   cup (2 oz.) dry white wine
½   teaspoon paprika
2   tablespoons olive oil
1   tablespoon butter
1¾   cups chicken broth
2   cups milk
Salt to taste
Freshly ground pepper
Croutons for garnish

In a large casserole, bring 1 cup water to a boil and add the escarole. Cover and cook over medium heat for about 5 minutes or until tender. Remove and drain.

In a food processor or blender (a little at a time if necessary), mix the escarole, garlic, wine, and paprika until smooth. Set aside.

Heat the oil and butter in the casserole and sauté the onions until soft. Add the broth, milk, the blender mixture, and salt and pepper to taste. Mix well. Bring just to the boiling point over medium heat.

Serve hot in individual soup bowls, sprinkled with the croutons.

Egg Dishes / Tortillas

THREE-LAYER OMELET
TORTILLA DE TRES HISTORIAS

This omelet dish is really three different taste creations in one. The first is a meat flavor, the second a tomato taste, and the third is the sweet, unmistakable flavor of pimento. Cover it with melted cheese and it's a simple feast.

SERVES 4

6	tablespoons olive oil
6	eggs or egg substitute equivalent
2	tablespoons chopped chorizo
2	tablespoons chopped serrano or prosciutto ham
2	tablespoons chopped onion
1	clove garlic, peeled and mashed
3	tablespoons chopped tomato
4	small pitted green olives, chopped
3	tablespoons chopped celery
1	tablespoon chopped flat parsley
2	tablespoons chopped canned pimento
	Salt to taste
	Freshly ground pepper
2	slices Muenster cheese
2	orange slices for garnish
1	sprig parsley for garnish

In a 9-inch skillet, heat 2 tablespoons olive oil over medium heat and add 2 beaten eggs. Sprinkle in the chorizo, ham, and chopped onion. Cook until eggs are completely set. Remove to a serving platter and keep warm.

In the same skillet, add 2 more tablespoons olive oil and sauté the garlic for about a minute. Add 2 more beaten eggs. Sprinkle in the tomato, olives, and celery. Cook until the eggs are completely set. Remove and place this on top of the first omelet.

In the same skillet, heat the last 2 tablespoons olive oil. Add 2 remaining beaten eggs and sprinkle in the parsley, pimento, and salt and pepper to taste. Cook until eggs are completely set. Remove and place on top of the second omelet.

Cover the top omelet with the cheese. Place all three stacked omelets under a broiler until cheese has melted. Remove from broiler carefully — the plate will be hot. Set the hot plate on top of a larger cold platter.

Garnish the top with orange slices and parsley sprigs. Serve in wedges.

Rice / Arrozes

CHICKEN AND SAUSAGE PAELLA
PAELLA ESTILO CATALÁN

Paella dishes are as varied as the cooks who create them. This particular version is served at the Parador Duques de Cardona on top of a mountain near Barcelona. The combination of sausage, ham, and chicken is especially hearty and full of flavor. No less than you'd expect from a mountaintop chef.

SERVES 6–8

3	pounds chicken, cut into serving pieces
	Salt to taste
	Freshly ground pepper
1½	pounds butifarra or sweet Italian sausages, cut into pieces
5	cloves garlic, mashed
1	large onion, peeled and chopped
3	tablespoons fresh chopped cilantro
¼	cup chopped serrano or prosciutto ham
4½	cups chicken broth

½ cup (4 oz.) dry white wine
¾ cup coarsely chopped carrots
2½ cups uncooked short- or long-grain rice
¼ cup frozen peas
8 strips canned pimento for garnish
4 sprigs parsley for garnish

Sprinkle the chicken with salt and pepper and rub well.

In a large paella pan, heat the oil and sauté the chicken pieces until golden. Remove and set aside.

In the same pan, sauté the sausages until golden color; remove and set aside. Pour off some of the oil, leaving 4 tablespoons oil in the pan. Add the garlic, onion, cilantro, and ham and sauté until onion is wilted. Add the broth, wine, and carrots and bring to a boil. Add the rice, and salt and pepper to taste. Mix well, cook uncovered for about 20 minutes or until the rice is semi-dry but some liquid remains. Arrange the chicken and sausages in the pan, buried halfway in the rice. Sprinkle the peas on top. Bake in a 325°F preheated oven for about 15 minutes or until the rice is dry. Remove the pan to a heat-resistant surface and garnish with the pimentos and parsley sprigs.

Shellfish / Mariscos

LOBSTER AND CHICKEN
LANGOSTA Y POLLO ESTILO CATALÁN

This recipe was developed around the turn of the century in the area of Costa Brava. It represents the finest traditions of Catalán cuisine, which historically has been very imaginative and unique. The chocolate and nuts with brandy and wine combined with rich lobster and tender chicken is a taste rarely found anywhere. This is an exotic dish.

SERVES 4

2 whole boneless breasts of chicken, split (about 1 lb.)
   Salt to taste
   Freshly ground pepper

¼   cup olive oil
4   lobster tails (about 6 oz. each), split lengthwise
1   medium chopped onion
3   tablespoons minced flat parsley
2   bay leaves
½   teaspoon thyme
½   pound fresh tomatoes, chopped
1   cup (8 oz.) dry white wine
3   tablespoons brandy
½   teaspoon crumbled saffron
6   cloves garlic, peeled
16   roasted almonds
½   cup walnut pieces
1½   teaspoons grated sweet chocolate
1   cup lobster or clam broth
2   sprigs parsley for garnish
4   orange slices for garnish

Sprinkle the chicken with salt and pepper and set aside.

In a large skillet, heat the oil and sauté the chicken and lobster until lobster is pink and chicken golden. Remove to a warm platter. In the same skillet, sauté the onion, 1 tablespoon minced parsley, bay leaves, thyme, tomatoes, wine, brandy, and salt and pepper to taste. Mix well, cover, and cook over medium-high heat for about 5–10 minutes. Add the lobster and chicken to the mixture, cover, and cook for about 5–10 more minutes.

In a food processor or blender, combine the saffron, garlic, almonds, walnuts, the remaining minced parsley, chocolate, and broth. Blend until smooth.

Pour the blender mixture over the lobster and chicken. Check for seasonings and continue cooking for about 5–10 more minutes. Discard bay leaves.

Transfer the lobster, chicken, and mixture to a serving platter and garnish with parsley sprigs and orange slices.

Serve this dish over your favorite pasta with a green salad.

SHELLFISH MEDLEY IN SAFFRON SAUCE
ZARZUELA

Zarzuela means a variety show, and this dish is certainly a variety of tastes. Introducing shrimp. Presenting lobster. Bring on the vegetables. Let's have a hand for the spices. Let's hear it for the clams and scallops. And now the finale, everything together in one unforgettable dish. Bravo!

SERVES 4

¼	cup olive oil
2	tablespoons butter
16	jumbo shrimp, shelled and deveined
2	lobster tails, split lengthwise
4	cloves garlic
1	medium onion, peeled and chopped
3	tablespoons chopped fresh cilantro
2	cups canned crushed tomatoes
¾	cup (6 oz.) dry white wine
2	tablespoons (1 oz.) brandy
½	cup fish broth
2	bay leaves
½	teaspoon crumbled saffron
1	teaspoon paprika
½	teaspoon crushed red pepper
	Salt to taste
12	small clams, well scrubbed
12	large sea scallops
2	lemon slices for garnish
2	lime slices for garnish
2	orange slices for garnish

In a large casserole, heat the oil and butter and sauté the shrimp and lobster until they turn pink. Remove and set aside.

In the same casserole, sauté the garlic, onion, and cilantro until onion is soft. Add the tomatoes, wine, brandy, broth, bay leaves, saffron, paprika, crushed red pepper, and salt to taste. Bring to a boil and cook uncovered over low heat for about 15 minutes. Add the clams, cover, and continue cooking over low heat until clams have opened. Return the lobster and shrimp to the casserole and add the scallops. Cook uncovered for about 5 minutes or until the scallops are done. Discard bay leaves.

Remove the shellfish to a deep serving platter and pour the sauce over it. Garnish with slices of lemon, lime, and orange.

Serve with white rice.

LOBSTER IN ROMESCO SAUCE
LANGOSTA A LA ROMESCO

The Catalans expect every chef to create his or her own version of Romesco sauce, based on tradition that basically calls for garlic, nuts, wine, and crushed red pepper. So tie on your apron, split a few lobster tails, and create Romesco.

SERVES 4

¼	cup olive oil
8	small lobster tails, cut lengthwise
4	sprigs parsley for garnish
4	orange slices for garnish

ROMESCO SAUCE

3	cloves garlic, peeled
¼	cup ground blanched almonds
¼	cup ground blanched hazelnuts
½	cup chopped onion
1	tablespoon chopped fresh cilantro
¼	cup (2 oz.) dry white wine
½	teaspoon crushed red pepper
1½	cups fish broth
2	slices bread, crusts removed
¼	teaspoon oregano
1	canned whole pimento, chopped
½	cup canned crushed tomatoes
1	teaspoon salt
¼	cup virgin olive oil

In a large casserole, heat ¼ cup oil and sauté lobster until it turns pink. Remove and set aside.

In a food processor or blender, mix all the ingredients for the Romesco (a little at a time, if necessary), and blend until smooth. Pour the mixture into the casserole and mix well. Cover and cook over low heat for about 10 minutes. Return the lobster to the casserole and continue cooking until lobster is done.

Remove lobster and sauce to a serving platter and garnish with parsley sprigs and orange slices.

Great partners for this dish are hot, crunchy bread and a green salad.

Fish / Pescado

BAKED RED SNAPPER FILLETS
PARGO A LA GERONA

I served this Catalán dish in my restaurant. It is also served in Barcelona at the Restaurante de Siete Portes. Red snapper is always a delightful, tasty fish. The white wine marinade adds a special flavor that is both subtle and distinct. All in all this dish is a favorite among the international travelers who visit this wonderful restaurant in Barcelona.

SERVES 4

4	red snapper fillets (about 6–8 oz. each)
¾	cup virgin olive oil
2	cloves garlic, peeled and mashed
¼	teaspoon salt
2	teaspoons chopped flat parsley
3	tablespoons dry white wine
1	teaspoon fish broth
4	lemon slices for garnish
4	sprigs parsley for garnish
½	teaspoon paprika for garnish

Place the fish in a flat-bottomed bowl and set aside.

In a medium mixing bowl, combine the oil, garlic, salt, chopped parsley, wine, and broth. Blend well with a whisk. Pour this mixture over the fish and rub well. Set aside for about 20 minutes.

Remove the fish from the marinade and drain. Place the fish in a baking pan and bake in a 350°F preheated oven for about 20 minutes or until the fish is done. Remove to a serving platter and pour some of the pan juices over the fish.

Garnish with lemon slices and parsley sprigs and sprinkle with paprika.

Serve with Mixed Vegetables, Castile Style and a baked potato.

ANGLER FISH IN SAFFRON AND GARLIC
RAPÉ ESTILO COSTA BRAVA

This delicious white fish cooked in white wine with white beans is very white—subtle, interesting, and delicate. Then you add the saffron and this beautiful white dish turns beautifully gold.

SERVES 4

¼ cup olive oil
1 large onion, coarsely chopped
1 large green bell pepper, seeded and coarsely chopped
¼ cup chopped fresh cilantro
1 cup (8 oz.) dry white wine
2 pounds angler fish, cut into round pieces
2 cups canned butter beans, drained
   Salt to taste
   Freshly ground pepper
4 cloves garlic, peeled
¾ cup clam broth
½ teaspoon cornstarch
½ teaspoon crumbled saffron
3 orange slices for garnish
3 sprigs parsley for garnish

In a large skillet, heat the oil and sauté the onion, bell pepper, and cilantro until onion is soft. Add the wine, fish, beans, and salt and pepper to taste. Cover and cook over low heat for about 15 minutes.

Meanwhile, in a food processor or blender, mix the garlic, broth, cornstarch, and saffron and blend until smooth.

Pour the mixture over the fish and continue cooking covered until fish is done. Remove the fish and mixture to a serving platter. Garnish with orange slices and parsley sprigs.

Serve with broccoli and papas fritas (fried potatoes).

Poultry / Aves

BAKED CHICKEN WITH HONEY
POLLO HORNEADO CON MIEL

You can make this dish according to the recipe, or you can fly free and broil the marinated chicken on the barbecue. It's muy rustico *and makes a great recipe even better.*

SERVES 4

3	pounds chicken, cut into quarters
3	orange slices for garnish
3	sprigs parsley for garnish

MARINADE
3	cloves garlic, peeled
3	tablespoons chopped onion
¼	teaspoon paprika
½	teaspoon lemon juice
2	teaspoons ground cumin
1½	tablespoons white vinegar
¼	cup honey
1	teaspoon salt (or less)
¾	cup olive oil

In a food processor or blender, add all the ingredients for the marinade and mix until smooth. Place the chicken pieces in a flat bowl and cover with the marinade. Rub well and set aside for about 2 hours in refrigerator.

Place the chicken pieces in a baking pan. Bake in a 350°F preheated oven, basting with the marinade every 20 minutes, for about 1 hour or until the chicken is done.

Remove to a serving platter and garnish with orange slices and parsley sprigs.

Serve this dish with Cucumber Salad.

CHICKEN WITH FRUITS
POLLO CON FRUTAS

The combination of chicken and fruit is typically Catalán. This dish dates back to 1477, another creation from Maestro Ruperto de Nola. You can create your own version, like I did, with fruits of your choice. Then set it before your king or queen, like Ruperto did.

SERVES 4

1	cup orange juice
2	tablespoons (1 oz.) brandy
¼	cup orange-blossom honey
2	tablespoons lemon juice
½	teaspoon paprika
1	teaspoon salt
3	tablespoons olive oil
2	tablespoons butter
3	pounds chicken, cut into serving pieces
12	canned pitted prunes, drained
8	canned peach halves, drained
¾	cup raisins
3	sprigs parsley for garnish
3	orange slices for garnish

In a medium mixing bowl, combine the orange juice, brandy, honey, lemon juice, paprika, and salt. Mix well until smooth and set aside.

In a large skillet, heat the oil and butter and sauté the chicken pieces until golden on all sides. Remove and drain. Dip the chicken pieces into the orange juice mixture and place them in a baking pan. Pour the juice mixture over the chicken and arrange the prunes, peaches, and raisins in the juice.

Cover the pan with foil and bake in a 350°F preheated oven for about 20 minutes or until the chicken is tender (be careful of steam when removing the foil).

Remove the chicken and fruits to a serving platter. Pour some of the sauce over the chicken and garnish with parsley sprigs and orange slices. *Serve with white rice and a green leafy vegetable.*

Meat / Carnes

BROILED STEAKS IN GARLIC SAUCE
ENTRECOTE AL AJILLO

Go to a restaurant. Order a sirloin steak. The cook throws it on the fire. Burns it. Serves it. And you eat it. Go see your butcher instead. Order a porterhouse or sirloin steak. Baste it with the special marinade you create with this recipe. Broil it. Baste it. Now you're eating steak al ajillo.

SERVES 4

GARLIC SAUCE
3	cloves garlic, peeled
3	tablespoons chopped onion
¼	teaspoon Tabasco sauce
½	teaspoon paprika
2	tablespoons (1 oz.) dry sherry
1	teaspoon fresh cilantro
1	teaspoon tomato sauce
2	tablespoons beef broth
½	cup olive oil
	Salt to taste
	Freshly ground pepper

4	sirloin or porterhouse steaks about 1½ inches thick
4	sprigs parsley for garnish

In a food processor or blender, mix all the same ingredients and blend until smooth. Pour the mixture into a small bowl and set aside.

Brush the steaks with the marinade on both sides and set aside for about 20 minutes. Reserve the rest of the marinade for later use. Transfer the steaks to a broiler pan with a grill and place it under the broiler. Cook until steaks are done to your satisfaction, turning once and basting with the reserved marinade.

Remove to a serving platter and garnish with parsley sprigs.

Serve with a baked potato or one of my Spanish rices.

BEEF WITH MIXED FRUITS
CARNE CON FRUTAS MIXTAS

Mixed fruit recipes are traditional Catalán dishes. Of course, I make my own versions and you can, too. And if you'd like to add a touch of brandy to the beef and fruit, please do! There are no rules.

SERVES 4

2	pounds lean beef, cut into 2-inch cubes
	Salt to taste
	Freshly ground pepper
¾	cup water
½	cup (4 oz.) red wine
2	tablespoons (1 oz.) brandy
3	tablespoons sugar
¼	cup cream
6	dried apricots
6	dried prunes
6	dried dates
6	dried figs
1	teaspoon salt (or less)
¼	cup olive oil
4	orange slices for garnish

Sprinkle the meat with salt and pepper. Rub well and set aside.

In a medium saucepan, combine the water, wine, brandy, sugar, cream, dried fruits, and salt to taste. Mix well. Cover and cook over low heat for about 30 minutes or until the fruits are almost soft. Set aside.

In a large skillet, heat the oil and sauté the meat until brown on all sides. Remove the skillet from the stove and pour the fruit mixture into the skillet. Check for seasoning and mix well. Cover and cook over low heat for about 30 minutes or until the meat is tender.

Remove the meat and fruit mixture to a serving platter and garnish with orange slices.

This dish can be served with Saffron Rice.

PORK CHOPS IN APPLE AND BRANDY SAUCE
CHULETAS DE CERDO A LA BARCELONA

This dish comes from the popular La Balsa Restaurant in Barcelona. Apples and pork are common everywhere, but this special double-boiler brandy sauce creates an aroma and flavor that you and your dinner guests will long remember. Gracias, Mercedes Lopes, for your recipe.

SERVES 4

SAUCE
- 2 cloves garlic, peeled and chopped
- ¾ cup applesauce
- 1 teaspoon lime juice
- 1 teaspoon salt (or less)
- ¼ cup water
- 2 tablespoons olive oil
- 2 tablespoons sugar
- 1 tablespoon brandy
- 1 teaspoon chopped flat parsley

- ¼ cup olive oil
- 4 center-cut pork chops
- ¼ cup (2 oz.) dry white wine
- ¼ cup chopped apple for garnish
- 4 sprigs parsley for garnish

In a food processor or blender, mix all the sauce ingredients and blend well until smooth. Transfer the mixture to a double boiler and keep warm for later use.

In a large skillet, heat ¼ cup oil and sauté the pork chops on both sides until light golden. Add the wine; cover and cook over low heat until pork chops are done, about 20 minutes.

Remove the pork chops to a serving platter and pour the sauce from the double boiler over them. Garnish with chopped apples and parsley sprigs.

Serve this dish with baked potato or one of my special Spanish rices.

Desserts / Postres

ORANGE CUSTARD FLAN
FLAN DE NARANJA A LA CATALANA

This is not a simple recipe, but it is a great dessert. You can do it. Caramelize the pan. Mix well. Mix well again. And mix again. Then bake. Then chill. Or you can visit Barcelona and enjoy this wonderful dessert with a cup of coffee at a café on La Rambla.

SERVES 8

1	cup sugar for caramelization
1	tablespoon water
2	teaspoons cornstarch
¼	teaspoon salt
2	cups orange juice
8	eggs, lightly beaten
2¼	cups fine sugar

Caramelize an 8-inch round baking pan 3 inches deep (without the tube) with 1 cup sugar and 1 tablespoon water. Cover the bottom and sides of the pan with the caramel and set aside.

In a medium saucepan, mix the cornstarch, salt, and 1 cup of the orange juice. Blend well until smooth. Add the eggs and mix well. Add the sugar and the rest of the orange juice. Mix well until sugar dissolves. Pour the mixture through a strainer into the caramelized pan. Place the pan inside a larger pan containing water to a depth of about 1 inch. Bake in a 350°F preheated oven for about 1 hour or until the custard is golden. Remove the custard pan from the pan of water and cool at room temperature. Transfer the pan of custard to the refrigerator and chill.

To unmold, place a serving plate over the pan and flip it over.

ORANGE CAKE SQUARES
TORTITAS DE NARANJAS

This is a simple recipe and a delightful dessert. You can follow the recipe as is or use your favorite fruit filling to create your own special taste. In Catalonia there is so much fruit available all year long, this dessert can be prepared dozens of ways.

SERVES 4

1	cup flour
½	cup melted butter
¼	cup confectioner's sugar for dusting

FILLING
2	eggs, lightly beaten
¾	cup sugar
2	teaspoons sifted flour
½	teaspoon baking powder
2	tablespoons orange juice
2	teaspoons lemon juice
½	teaspoon grated orange peel

In a mixing bowl, combine 1 cup flour and the butter. Mix well until a dough ball is formed. Transfer the dough to a working surface and flatten it with the heel of your hand. Place the dough in an 8-inch square buttered baking pan and with your fingers press the dough to the sides of the pan. Bake in a 350°F preheated oven for about 12 to 15 minutes or until the dough begins to turn golden.

Meanwhile, in a food processor or blender, mix all the ingredients for the filling until smooth. Pour the mixture over the dough and continue baking for about 20 minutes more.

Sprinkle with confectioner's sugar. Cut into squares to serve.

Mallorca

THE BALEARIC
ISLANDS

The Balearic Islands are Spanish picture postcards. Of the four islands, Mallorca is the major one, Minorca a minor one, and Formentera and Ibiza two of the most beautiful, beachy islands found anywhere in the world. The islands were dominated by the Moorish invaders, and it was not until the thirteenth century that a Spanish fleet flying the flag of the king of Aragón regained the islands for the Aragón-Catalonian Alliance. The islands remained Spanish and undisturbed until the chic *elegantes* of Europe and the hippie world travelers of the early 1960s simultaneously made Formentera and Ibiza "the" places to experience. Beautiful beaches in all colors, palm trees, and pine-covered gentle mountains create a perfect setting for travelers seeking refuge from their imperfect worlds.

Mallorca is basically Palma, a city of Old World grace and stately mansions left over from the Arab and Spanish royalty eras. The city boasts an international airport along with its giant Gothic cathedral and quaint winding alleys that reveal old homes and charming restaurants that specialize in native dishes. Outside of the city and fronting the Mallorcan beaches are hotels, apartments, and the busy clubs and nightspots that are part of an international fun city.

Unlike Mallorca, Formentera and Ibiza are dotted with immaculately maintained snow-white stucco cottages topped with red-tile roofs. The quiet hillsides are abundant with groves of almonds, figs, and olives, marks of the Moorish occupation. The island peace is unruffled by jet planes and condominiums.

Minorca is even more simple. Geographically plain and hardly industrious, the Minorcans concentrate on their fields of beautiful vegetables and luscious fruit. The island's splendor is its natural setting in crystal-clear Mediterranean water and a sparkling sun that nourishes the people and their crops.

Minorca's capital city of Mahón is famous as the locale for one of the Balearic culinary legends. The story, offered as fact, tells of a royal chef who ran out of butter during his preparation of a dressing for the royal dinner. His imagination seized upon olive oil, basic to all Spanish cuisine, and combining it with eggs, vinegar, spices, and a tireless whisk, he created mayonnaise. Sometimes unaccepted but never disproved, the story reinforces the classic history of Spanish cooking that predates most of Europe's culinary creations.

Fresh fish and seafood is the mark of great Balearic cuisine. Squid, lobster, shrimp, crayfish, mussels, octopus, and fish in amazing variety are so delicious they give new meaning to the word "fresh." Fish arrives every day from boat to table. No trucks, freezers, processors, or canners come between the diner and the best seafood available anywhere. This ocean harvest combined with the Spanish culinary imagination creates seafood prepared with raisins, pine nuts, eggs, cream sauces, exotic spices, and marinades. It is a far cry from the simply baked, quickly broiled, and crusty fried fish dishes of most of the world.

Seafood is accompanied by a wonderful variety of fresh vegetables. Of course, everything in Spain's vegetable array starts with tomatoes, onions, and garlic. In the Balearics add spinach, asparagus, red peppers, green and yellow zucchini, hard-skinned squashes, and soft-skinned olives. Fruit is both staple and exotic. The beautiful groves provide oranges, pears, and bananas along with pomegranates, cactus pear, figs, lichee, and melons of every color flesh.

If nature does her part to make the Balearic table a feasting place, so does the Balearic pastry chef. Sweet cakes, buns, and rolls are available everywhere at all times. Breakfast is a tray of pastries and sweet rolls with hot coffee, chocolate, and orange juice. Puff pastry filled with apricot marmalade, almond paste, or banana custard is a perfect dessert—unless, of course, you choose an Arab almond tart or a slice of Flaon, a cheesecake flavored with mint, anisette, and honey created by Spain's master chef Ruperto de Nola as recorded in his second cookbook published in 1525.

The Balearic Islands will satisfy your desire for sun, sand, and sea. The Balearic cuisine will spark a new desire for food that is skill-fully prepared with the freshest ingredients, traditional recipes, and un-limited imagination.

THE WINES OF THE BALEARIC ISLANDS

The Balearic Islands import far more wine than they produce. The history of Balearic winemaking begins with the Romans and ends with the plague of the late 1800s. Great food, however, deserves great wine companions, and the abundance of world-class wines from Rioja, Catalonia, and Andalucía will enhance and complete your Balearic culinary experience.

Appetizers / Tapas

MINIATURE PIZZAS
COCAS MALLORQUINAS

This is one of the best-known specialties of the islands. Originally this recipe called for using bread dough and embedding finely chopped onions in it before rolling it into 6-inch rounds. I suggest a much simpler way to prepare these cocas. *Use 6- or 8-inch flour tortillas, which are available in most supermarkets, to create a lighter, less doughy pizza. So what are you waiting for?*

SERVES 4

4   flour tortillas, 6 or 8 inches in diameter
6   tablespoons olive oil
2   cloves garlic, mashed
1   tablespoon chopped fresh cilantro
1   small tomato, thinly sliced
1   small onion, thinly sliced
     Salt to taste
     Freshly ground pepper

Place the tortillas on an oiled or buttered cookie sheet and set aside.

In a food processor or blender, mix the olive oil, garlic, and cilantro and blend until smooth. Brush the mixture onto the tortillas. Place 3 or 4 slices of tomato and onion on each tortilla to cover most of it. Sprinkle with salt and pepper to taste and bake in 350°F preheated oven for about 10 minutes.

BAKED CLAMS WITH RUM
ALMEJAS AL RON

This is a simple recipe with an exciting flavor. Clams are an island favorite. So is rum. Together they are wonderful companions. The stuffing is easy and the results are sabor especial.

SERVES 4

12   large clams, washed and scrubbed
12   pimento strips for garnish

STUFFING
  2   cloves garlic, peeled
¼   cup ground walnuts
  2   tablespoons chopped scallions
¼   teaspoon salt (or less)
¼   teaspoon paprika
  2   tablespoons (1 oz.) dark rum
  1   tablespoon bread crumbs

Open the clams with a clam knife; discard the empty halves of the shells and save the juices for future use. Place the half-shell clams in an oiled or buttered baking pan and set aside.

In a food processor or blender, mix all the ingredients for the stuffing and blend until smooth. Fill each shell with the mixture and bake in a 375°F preheated oven for about 10 minutes or until the mixture is golden.

Remove and garnish with the pimento strips.

HOT GARLIC MAYONNAISE WITH POTATOES
PATATAS CON MAHONESA PICANTE

Legend has it that in the year 1757 a chef working in the port city of Mahón, capital of Minorca, was preparing a butter sauce. He ran out of butter. So he improvised, using olive oil in place of the butter. To his amazement and delight he produced a creamy, smooth, sweet dressing. He had created mayonnaise. A new dressing and a new name from the Spanish port of Mahón.

SERVES 4

  4   cups water
¼   teaspoon salt (or less)
  4   medium white potatoes, peeled, washed, and cut into
          chunks
  3   tablespoons chopped parsley for garnish

MAYONNAISE
4   cloves garlic, peeled
1   egg yolk
2   tablespoons chopped onion
3   tablespoons chopped fresh cilantro
⅛   teaspoon cayenne pepper
1   teaspoon lemon juice
1   teaspoon vinegar
½   teaspoon salt (or less)
1   cup olive oil

In a large saucepan, bring the water and salt to a boil. Place the potatoes in the water and boil for about 20 minutes or until the potatoes are soft. Remove the potatoes and rinse with cold water and drain. Remove to a large bowl and set aside.

In a food processor or blender, mix all the ingredients for the mayonnaise except the oil and blend well until smooth. (When making any sauce or mayonnaise, if it begins to break down during the mixing, don't despair. Simply add 1 or 2 tablespoons of hot water and continue mixing slowly.) With the motor running, add the oil in a thin stream until the mixture is creamy. Pour the mixture over the potatoes and mix well.

Serve at room temperature and garnish with chopped parsley.

Vegetables / Legumbres

ONIONS STUFFED WITH SHRIMP
CEBOLLAS RELLENAS

This dish is a winner. It comes from the Valparaiso Restaurant in Palma, which specializes in authentic regional cooking like this stuffed onion recipe native to the islands. I have added a touch of brandy for extra flavor. You can create your own version of a stuffing as well. It is the onion "cups" that really make this dish. It's a wonderful presentation.

SERVES 4

4   large Spanish onions, peeled and boiled for about 20
      minutes
    Butter
3   tablespoons chopped parsley for garnish

STUFFING
¾   cup chopped cooked shrimp
¼   cup chopped serrano or prosciutto ham
2   cups seasoned bread crumbs
1   clove garlic, peeled
3   tablespoons chopped fresh cilantro
¼   teaspoon salt (or less)
1   teaspoon brandy
¾   cup canned crushed tomatoes

Cut a large slice from the top of each onion (discard) and scoop out the center to make a cup, leaving about ½ inch of wall. Reserve 1 cup of the scooped onion and place the onion cups in an oiled or buttered baking pan with about ½ cup water. Set aside.

In a food processor or blender, mix the stuffing ingredients plus the reserved scooped onion and blend until a smooth paste has formed.

Fill the cups with the mixture, dot with butter, and bake in a 375°F preheated oven for about 25 minutes or until the tops have turned golden.

Remove to a serving platter and sprinkle with chopped parsley.
Serve with a side dish of mashed potatoes or Saffron Rice.

Salads / Ensaladas

APPLE AND PEPPER SALAD
ENSALADA ESTILO MALLORCA

Many of the native dishes of the Balearic Islands are based on the local abundance of excellent vegetables. Although this particular dish has its early roots in Catalonia, it represents the style and character of many Balearic recipes. I suggest small, dark red cherry tomatoes for their sweetness, and celery is an excellent substitute for the green pepper. This dish has what I like in almost any salad: lots of texture, varied tastes, and sweet/sharp contrasts.

SERVES 4

10	firm cherry tomatoes, cut in halves
2	green medium apples, peeled, seeded, and coarsely chopped
1	large red bell pepper, seeded and coarsely chopped
1	large green bell pepper, seeded and coarsely chopped
2	small onions, peeled and thinly sliced
¼	cup raisins, soaked in water and drained
2	tablespoons orange juice
¼	teaspoon salt (or less)
	Freshly ground pepper
½	cup extra virgin olive oil
4	orange slices for garnish

Place all ingredients except the garnish in a large salad bowl. Mix well and set aside for about 30 minutes before serving.

Transfer to individual salad bowls and garnish with orange slices.

Soups / Sopas

CABBAGE SOUP
SOPA AL ESTILO DE MALLORCA

This is the most famous soup of the Balearic Islands. It is made with island produce: onions, cabbage, fresh vegetables, and a touch of dry sherry. That's my idea. Good, no? The toast and grated cheese are also excellent touches that contribute to the pleasure of this soup.

SERVES 4

4	cloves garlic, peeled
1	bay leaf
1	large green bell pepper, seeded and chopped

   2   cups canned whole tomatoes, drained
   3   tablespoons olive oil
   3   tablespoons butter
   1   large onion, peeled and finely chopped
   4   cups beef or chicken broth
   ¼   cup (2 oz.) dry sherry
   3   tablespoons chopped flat parsley
   1   small head of cabbage (1 lb.), shredded
   ¼   teaspoon freshly ground pepper
       Salt to taste
   4   slices toasted French bread for garnish
   4   teaspoons grated Parmesan cheese for garnish

In a food processor or blender, mix the garlic, bay leaf, green pepper, and tomatoes. Blend until smooth. Reserve.

In a large casserole, heat the oil and butter and sauté the onion until golden. Add the broth, sherry, parsley, cabbage, the reserved mixture, ground pepper, and salt to taste. Mix well. Cover and cook over medium-high heat for about 30 minutes, or until cabbage is soft.

Transfer to individual soup bowls and garnish with the toast and grated cheese.

LOBSTER SOUP WITH TOMATOES
SOPA DE LANGOSTA CON TOMATES

This marriage of lobster, tomatoes, and cilantro is characterized by a flavor that is mellow, sweet, and sharp. The recipe was given to me by El Gallo Restaurant, located in the city of Palma de Mallorca. I guarantee you this is a sure winner. Bet all you've got.

SERVES 4 – 6

   ¼   cup olive oil
   5   cloves garlic, peeled and mashed
   2   large onions, peeled and chopped
   4   tablespoons chopped fresh cilantro
   2   small green bell peppers, seeded and chopped
   2   bay leaves, crumbled
   2   cups canned crushed tomatoes
   ¼   cup (2 oz.) dry sherry

2   cups clam broth
2   cups chicken broth
2   medium carrots, peeled and cut into large pieces
     Salt to taste
     Freshly ground pepper
2   lobster tails, shelled and sliced
1   tablespoon chopped parsley for garnish
4   lemon slices for garnish

In a large deep casserole, heat the oil and sauté the garlic, onion, cilantro, green peppers, and bay leaves until onion is soft. Add the tomatoes, sherry, clam and chicken broths, carrots, and salt and pepper to taste. Mix well and bring to a boil. Cover and cook over medium-low heat for about 30 minutes or until the carrots are soft. Add the lobster and continue cooking, uncovered, for about 10 minutes or until the lobster is done.

Remove to individual soup bowls and garnish with chopped parsley and lemon slices.

Shellfish / Mariscos

SHRIMP WITH WALNUTS
GAMBAS A LA MALLORCA

The Balearic Islands produce almonds, walnuts, olives, raisins, and superb fruit. This dish is a blend of these beautiful things together with fresh shrimp from the Mediterranean Sea.

SERVES 4

½   cup (4 oz.) olive oil
2   medium onions, peeled and chopped
3   tablespoons chopped flat parsley
1   teaspoon paprika
8   medium tomatoes, peeled, seeded, and coarsely
        chopped
½   cup (4 oz.) dry white wine

¼   cup ground walnuts
¼   cup raisins
      Salt to taste
      Freshly ground pepper
2   pounds large shrimp, shelled and cleaned
¼   cup (2 oz.) brandy
3   orange slices for garnish
3   sprigs parsley for garnish

In a large skillet, heat the oil and sauté the onions, parsley, and paprika until onion is soft. Add the tomatoes, wine, walnuts, raisins, and salt and pepper to taste. Mix well and bring to a boil. Cook, uncovered, over medium heat for about 15 minutes or until the sauce starts to thicken. Add the shrimp and brandy and continue cooking until shrimp is done.

Remove the shrimp and mixture to a serving platter and garnish with orange slices and parsley sprigs.

Serve with Potato Salad Valencia Style.

Desserts / Postres

ALMOND CUPCAKES
PASTELITOS DE ALMENDRAS

The restaurant Ancora in Palma de Majorca specializes in attractive sweet postres *like this cupcake. Many are complicated and require the skill and experience of master pastry chefs. These delicate cupcakes, however, are easy to prepare.*

MAKES ABOUT 4–6 CUPCAKES

3   eggs
4   tablespoons fine sugar
½   cup all-purpose flour
¼   teaspoon grated orange peel
¼   cup finely chopped almonds

Separate the egg yolks and whip the egg whites in a bowl until foamy. Add the yolks, sugar, flour, orange peel, and almonds and mix until a smooth paste forms. In a small buttered baking cupcake pan, fill each cup ¾ full with dough. Bake in a 350°F preheated oven for about 10 minutes or until done.

Remove from the oven and let cool.

CLASSIC CHEESECAKE
FLAON

This cheesecake recipe, called Flaon, *is one of the classical desserts prepared by Maestro Ruperto de Nola. You can find the recipe in his original cookbook,* Libre de Coch, *published in 1477, available through the Library of Congress Historical Collection. Of course, it was written in Catalán, but I have translated it for you into English. What a great idea.*

SERVES 6

1	cup all-purpose flour
	Dash salt
3	tablespoons water
3	tablespoons olive oil
½	pound ricotta cheese
2	eggs, beaten lightly
⅔	cup fine sugar
¼	teaspoon finely chopped fresh mint
⅛	teaspoon Licor 43
¼	cup orange-blossom honey
1½	teaspoons rose water
1	teaspoon ground nutmeg

Place the flour in a mixing bowl and add the salt, water, and oil. Mix well until a ball of dough is formed. Place the ball on a working surface and, with the heel of your hands, work the dough until it is flattened. Place the flattened dough in an 8-inch springform pan and with the tip of your fingers work the dough onto the sides of the pan. Set aside.

In a medium bowl, add the ricotta cheese, eggs, and sugar and mix well until smooth. Cover the top of the dough with the cheese mixture and bake in a 350°F preheated oven for about 30–40 minutes or until a toothpick is inserted and comes out dry. Remove from oven and set aside.

In a small saucepan, heat the honey and rose water over low heat. Drizzle it over the cake. Sprinkle the top of the cake with the ground nutmeg and set aside in a cool place.

Once the cake is baked, remove from the pan and serve at room temperature.

Dunes of Gran Canaria

THE CANARY
ISLANDS

There are no canaries on the Canary Islands other than a few specimens from pet shops kept by bird lovers. The islands are named for a breed of wild dogs found there more than a thousand years ago. There are seven Canary Islands, products of violent volcanic action that created this chain of unusual Atlantic islands off the coast of North Africa. Tenerife, the largest island, looks a lot like the moon, full of craters and black soil. Gran Canaria, the busiest of the islands, is home to Las Palmas, the capital city of the region.

The Canary Islands are a wonderful tourist attraction, with rocky beaches broken by sandy stretches that open to the Atlantic waves. Summer is short, but springtime lasts a long time. Life is shaped by the sea, and outside of the capital city the island life is quiet. Giant ferry boats carry tourists and their vehicles from Spain's Port Ceuta to Las Palmas. Visitors scurry about looking for typical native attractions, museums, cathedrals, and things Spanish. They find very little that meets those expectations. The Canaries are natural creations. Arabs, Moors, Italians, Portuguese, and Spanish adventurers all came to the islands, and they all left leaving little of their culture. It is the sea that rules the Canary Islands.

Housewives lean out their windows as the *vendero pescado* makes his way along the cobblestone streets leading his burro laden with great varieties of fish caught by the local *pescaderos*. The fish is always perfectly fresh and beautifully prepared. It is from the Atlantic waters, more difficult to fish than the clear Mediterranean or the northern bay of Spain, so varieties are somewhat limited. Squid is plentiful. So are squid recipes and the imagination that goes into stuffing them, broiling them, simmering them in tomato sauce, or frying them in fresh garlic and olive oil.

Produce is abundant in the Canaries. Strawberries, asparagus, greens, and tiny potatoes, said to be among the finest in the world, are plentiful and delicious. Sugar cane is raised; so is tobacco. (Gran Canaria has a major cigar industry.) But the major fruit of the Canary Islands is bananas. Bananas grow in profusion and were stored in the ships that sailed to Spanish America, where they became one of the major fruit products of the New World.

THE WINES OF THE CANARY ISLANDS

The wine history of the Canary Islands lies in the past and in the future. During the 1400s seafarers and conquistadores passed through the busy ports of the Canary Islands. Wine was a common pleasure, and although many varieties of grape were planted, it was one Fernando de Castro who introduced the Malvasia grape to the volcanic island of Tenerife. The combination of the hardy fruit with the mineral-rich volcanic soil and dry climate created a healthy grape which grew so profusely it allowed two pickings a season. The first picking was a green grape, slightly acid and bitter, but one that produced large volumes of liquid. Half the grapes were left to turn purple and ripe and were picked late in the season. This picking produced a liquid with more sugar, a mellow flavor, and high alcohol. The fermentation process took place in large, open casks and the blending of the first and second pressings produced a golden wine that was highly intoxicating, with hints of sweetness, acidity, and sharpness, all in one glass of wine. No wonder this Malvasian wine of the Canary Islands became internationally famous and was in great demand.

In the sixteenth century, the sugar cane industry was booming in the New World and the Alert Canarians replanted thousands of acres of sugar cane with grapevines. Thousands of casks of Canary Island wine were shipped everywhere: to the New World colonies, the Atlantic Coast countries of Africa, and throughout Europe, especially England and Holland. The wine industry became the single most important source of income for the islands. The winemaking became a national affair. It was said at the time, "one house, one bodega."

In addition to its great export wine industry, the Canary Islands introduced the grapevine to the New World. The hardy Canary root-stock resisted the phylloxera epidemic that destroyed the European vineyards. The rootstocks were replaced with American stock that originally came from the Canary Islands. It is a fact that most European vines live about thirty years while Canary Island and American vines live for sixty.

Despite the high-quality characteristics of both the Canary Island wines and rootstock and its enormous export industry, they were no match for several events that took place late in the 1600s.

Charles II of England, as part of the international struggle to control land and commerce in the New World, passed the Navigation Acts that prohibited trade with the New World by any people other than the British, and shipping to the New World could only be on British ships. An alliance with Portugal created a powerful maritime force combined with subsidized pirate activities that shifted the balance of naval, political, and economic power from Spain and Holland to England. At the same time, a two-part epidemic of oidium and mildew severely crippled the vineyard production. The Canary Islands lost their markets and their product at the same time. Thousands of acres on every island were replanted with bananas and coconuts, two fruits that were also introduced to the New World from the Canary Islands.

Only in the past decade, as the consumption and appreciation of fine Spanish wines have increased internationally, have the Canaries once again replanted their islands with their famous Malvasian grape. Old wood cask bodegas are being replaced by stainless-steel vats and modern technology. It is only a matter of time before we will once again select and enjoy one of the world's very special wines.

Vegetables / Legumbres

HOT POTATOES, CANARY STYLE
PAPAS ARRUGADAS

Everyplace you go in the Canary Islands, you are going to find this dish. It is an exceptional treat for real lovers of hot and spicy ingredients. And we don't call this recipe Hot Potatoes for nothing. Of course, if you are not into hot and spicy foods, use just a pinch of cayenne and crushed red pepper instead of the indicated amounts. Or even cooler, use sweet paprika instead.

SERVES 4

20   small new potatoes, scrubbed

SAUCE
4	cloves garlic, peeled
3	tablespoons chopped onion
½	teaspoon cayenne pepper
¼	teaspoon crushed red pepper
3	tablespoons chopped fresh cilantro
1	teaspoon ground cumin
½	cup red wine vinegar
½	teaspoon salt (or less)
¾	cup olive oil
3	orange slices for garnish

Place the potatoes in a large pot. Cover with water and bring to a boil. Cook uncovered for about 30 minutes or until the potatoes are tender. Drain, dry, and place them in an oiled or buttered baking pan. Bake in a 425°F preheated oven for about 10 minutes.

In a food processor or blender, mix all the ingredients for the sauce except the garnish. Blend well until smooth. Reserve.

Cut the potatoes in half and place them in a serving bowl. Pour the reserved sauce over them and mix well. Garnish with the orange slices and serve hot.

Rice / Arrozes

RICE WITH HAM AND BANANAS
ARROZ AL CANARIO

Bananas are native to the Canary Islands. It was from these tiny Spanish islands that the Western world received this versatile, common fruit. Bananas were introduced by the Spanish to the Americas around 1500 from expeditions that left the island of Gomera. This recipe of many ingredients will give you a wide variety of tastes. The ripe banana fairly bursts through the spices and flavors with its sweetness and smoothness.

SERVES 4 – 5

2	tablespoons olive oil
2	tablespoons butter
3	cloves garlic, peeled and mashed
1	medium onion, peeled and chopped
2	tablespoons chopped fresh cilantro
¼	cup chopped serrano or prosciutto ham
1	cup water
¼	cup grated dried coconut
2¾	cups chicken broth
¼	cup (2 oz.) white wine
¼	teaspoon hot paprika or cayenne
1	teaspoon salt (or less)
3	beaten eggs or egg substitute equivalent
2	cups uncooked rice
2	large ripe bananas, peeled and cut into 1-inch rounds
2	tablespoons chopped parsley for garnish
1	canned whole pimento for garnish

In a large casserole, heat the oil and butter and sauté the garlic, onion, cilantro, and ham until onion is soft. Add the water, coconut, broth, wine, hot paprika, and salt to taste. Mix well and bring to a boil. Add the eggs in a thin stream while mixing; then add the rice. Cook, uncovered, over medium-high heat for about 15 minutes or until the rice is semi-dry but some liquid remains. Cover and cook over low heat for about 20 minutes or until the rice is dry. Turn the rice over with a fork from bottom to top. Arrange the bananas over the rice. Sprinkle the parsley on top and place the pimento in the center. Cover and continue cooking for about 10 more minutes.

Serve with Tomatoes with Roncal Cheese.

Shellfish / Mariscos

LOBSTER IN CAPERS AND WINE
LANGOSTA LAS PALMAS

This is a recipe from El Acuario Restaurant in Las Palmas, where you select your own fresh lobster from a large tank. The recipe contains many spices and herbs along with the capers—a sophisticated variety of flavors. It will make you appreciate lobster as something more than boiled shellfish dipped in butter. This wonderful food from the sea deserves more. So do you.

SERVES 4

½   cup olive oil
6   cloves garlic, peeled and mashed
2   large onions, peeled and chopped
1   tablespoon chopped fresh cilantro
2   medium green bell peppers, seeded and chopped
2   cups tomato sauce
¼   teaspoon ground cumin
¼   teaspoon dried oregano
¼   teaspoon paprika
1   bay leaf
½   teaspoon crushed red pepper
10   small stuffed olives
½   teaspoon capers
½   teaspoon salt (or less)
¼   teaspoon freshly ground pepper
½   cup (4 oz.) red wine
4   medium lobster tails, split lengthwise
1   canned whole pimento, cut into strips for garnish

In a large casserole, heat the oil over medium-low heat and sauté the garlic, onions, cilantro, and green peppers until onion is soft. Add the tomato sauce, cumin, oregano, paprika, bay leaf, crushed red pepper, olives, capers, salt, and pepper. Mix well and bring to a boil. Add the wine and cook 1 minute. Add the lobster and continue cooking over medium-high heat, uncovered, for about 15 minutes or until the lobster is done. Discard bay leaf.

Remove the lobster to a serving platter, mix the sauce well, and pour over the lobster. Garnish with the pimento strips and serve.

Fish / Pescado

SOLE IN HOT PEPPER SAUCE
LENGUADO AL HIERRO

Island seafood is some of the best food in the world. When it's caught and prepared fresh like it always is in the Canaries and teamed with very hot spices that are a favorite with the Canarians, you are in for a treat. This recipe brings you the flavor of the islands. But like so many dishes from these islands, the key word is "hot." Maybe the natives are trying to appease the gods of Volcano Teide, which sits sleeping on the island of Tenerife. So use plenty of spice and maybe Teide will stay asleep.

SERVES 4

SAUCE
- 4   cloves garlic, peeled
- 3   tablespoons chopped onion
- 4   tablespoons chopped fresh cilantro
- 1   teaspoon paprika
- ½   teaspoon crushed red pepper
- ¼   teaspoon ground cumin
- 3   tablespoons sherry wine vinegar
- ½   teaspoon salt (or less)
- ¼   teaspoon freshly ground pepper
- ½   cup olive oil

    4   sole fillets (about 6–8 oz. each)
        Salt to taste
        Freshly ground pepper
        Flour for dusting
  ¼   cup olive oil
    2   tablespoons chopped parsley for garnish
    4   lemon slices for garnish

In a food processor or blender, combine all the ingredients for the sauce and blend until smooth. Set aside.

Sprinkle the sole fillets with salt and pepper and dust with flour. In a large skillet, heat the oil and sauté the fillets on both sides until done.

Transfer the fish to a serving platter and pour the blender mixture over them. Garnish with chopped parsley and lemon slices.

Serve with baked potato.

Poultry / Aves

LEMON AND CHICKEN
POLLO AL CANARIO

The Canary Islands were discovered by Juba, king of the Mauritanians, in 40 B.C. He named them the Canary Islands from the Latin word canes, *meaning canine, for the thousands of wild dogs that inhabited the islands. Today there are no wild dogs and no canaries. But there are plenty of chickens, and the spicy chefs of the Canaries prepare this lemon chicken recipe as good as any in the world. The sauce was made in spice heaven, and when the chickens and the mushrooms are sautéed together with all the flavors, something wonderful happens—you get to eat it.*

SERVES 4

    2   whole large breasts of chicken, halved
          (approx. 2 lb.)
        Salt
        Freshly ground pepper

       Flour for dusting
¼   cup olive oil
½   pound mushrooms, sliced
6   lemon slices for garnish
2   sprigs parsley for garnish

SAUCE
2   cloves garlic, peeled
1   small onion, peeled and coarsely chopped
1½ teaspoons salt (or less)
½   teaspoon cumin
½   teaspoon Dijon-style mustard
1   teaspoon sugar
½   teaspoon paprika
2   tablespoons chopped flat parsley
3   tablespoons lemon juice
½   tablespoon cornstarch
½   cup olive oil
¾   cup chicken broth

Sprinkle the chicken with salt and pepper, dust with flour, and set aside.

In a large skillet, heat the ¼ cup olive oil; sauté the chicken on both sides until golden. Remove to a warm platter.

In the same skillet, sauté the mushrooms for about 3 minutes and remove to a warm platter.

In a food processor or blender, mix all the ingredients for the sauce except the garnish and blend until smooth.

Return the chicken and mushrooms to the skillet and pour the sauce from the blender over them. Cook, uncovered, over medium-low heat for about 15 minutes or until the chicken is done.

Remove the chicken to a serving platter and pour the sauce and mushroom mixture over it. Garnish with lemon slices and parsley sprigs and serve hot.

Serve with Potato Salad Valencia Style.

Desserts / Postres

BANANAS WITH HONEY
PLÁTANOS CON MIEL

This is my mother's favorite dessert. Her family is native to the Canary Islands, where bananas are prepared dozens of ways—all good. Bananas were actually discovered in West Africa in the region called Banana (Ba-na-na') in Guinea. The fruit was named for the place it grew, but when it was introduced into Europe by the Portuguese, the accent moved to the second syllable, making it ba-na'-na. However you say it, this recipe is a special dessert treat. It is rich and smooth with the exciting taste of Licor 43 combined with honey and butter. My mother always makes this for me when I visit her. She makes the bananas ahead of time and chills them, because that's the way she likes them. Room temperature is okay, too. Whipped cream is also good. But hot is not.

SERVES 4

4	large bananas, peeled and split lengthwise
	Flour for dusting
¼	cup butter (or less)
½	cup honey
2	tablespoons water
1	tablespoon lemon juice
3	tablespoons Licor 43
1	teaspoon cinnamon powder

Dust the bananas with flour and set aside.

In a large skillet, melt the butter over medium heat and sauté the bananas for about 2 minutes, turning once.

Meanwhile, in a small bowl mix the honey, water, lemon juice, and liqueur. Pour over the bananas. Cook, uncovered, over low heat for about 3 minutes more.

Remove the bananas to a serving platter and pour the sauce over them. Sprinkle with cinnamon and serve chilled or at room temperature.

MENU SUGGESTIONS

REGIONAL MENUS

We Spanish love to eat . . . and eat often. The typical Spanish life-style includes a light breakfast at 8 A.M. or earlier, then a late breakfast, an early lunch snack, a late three-course lunch including wine and a dessert, a late-afternoon snack with sweets and coffee, followed by sherry and tapas at 8 P.M. as a prelude to a five- or six-course dinner at 10 P.M. or even later. As Spain evolves into modern times, this traditional eating pattern is changing. Still, mealtime is more frequent and more abundant than in most other countries. This book is based on classic Spanish cooking, but you can easily adopt Spanish menus and meals to suit your life-style and convenience. Following are some suggestions for complete meals and menus, but I encourage you to follow your own taste and imagination.

FROM LEVANTE

> Clams in Chili Sauce (Tapas)
> Pimento and Green Pepper Salad
> Dry, Full-Body Red Wine—Rioja
> Chicken and Shellfish Rice
> Oranges Caramelade
> Espresso Coffee

FROM ANDALUCÍA

> Dry Sherry—Jerez
> Mushrooms with Garlic (Tapas)
> Cold Tomato and Vegetable Soup
> Dry White Wine—Rioja
> Red Snapper in Sherry
> Cauliflower Muleteer Style
> Figs with Chocolate and Nuts
> Espresso Coffee with Orange Brandy Liqueur

FROM NEW CASTILE

> Stuffed Mussels with Ham (Tapas)
> Garlic Egg Soup Castilian Style
> Dry White Wine—Castilla y León
> Chicken and Almonds
> Vegetable Medley or Saffron Rice
> Rum Cake
> Coffee and Carlos I Brandy

FROM OLD CASTILE

> Dry Sherry (optional)—Jerez
> Mushrooms Segovia (Tapas)
> Dry, Full-Body Red Reserve—Rioja
> Pork Chops Rioja Style
> Potatoes in Vinegar Sauce
> Coffee and Walnut Cookies
> Sweet Sherry—Jerez

FROM NAVARRA AND ARAGÓN

> Tomatoes with Roncal Cheese
> Dry Light Red Wine—Aragón
> Chicken with Red Peppers
> White Rice and Sherry
> Peaches in Wine
> Espresso Coffee and Sweet Anise Liqueur

FROM CATALONIA

> Medium-Dry Sherry (optional)—Jerez
> Country Bread with Tomato and Ham (Tapas)
> Dry White Wine—Penedés
> Lobster and Chicken
> Catalán Style Spinach
> White Rice and Sherry
> Orange Custard Flan
> Coffee and Licor 43

FROM THE BASQUE COUNTRY

> Dry Sherry—Jerez
> Chorizos and Pears in Hard Cider (Tapas)

Cucumber Salad
Dry White Wine—Rioja
Fish and Clams in Parsley Sauce
White Rice with Dried Cod
Stewed Figs and Apricots
Espresso Coffee and Tres Torres Brandy

FROM EXTREMADURA

Medium-Dry Sherry (optional)—Jerez
Escarole with Olives and Cheese
White Gazpacho
Dry, Full-Body Red Reserve—Extremadura
Veal, Chorizo, and Peppers
Green Beans and Potatoes
Fried Bread with Brandy and Honey
Coffee

FROM ASTURIAS

Asparagus, Tuna, and Blue Cheese Salad
Hard Apple Cider "El Gaitero"—Asturias
Baked Hake and Shrimp in Hard Cider
Seafood-Flavored Rice and Sherry
Rice Pudding 43
Coffee

FROM THE CANARY ISLANDS

Mixed Vegetable Salad with Anchovy Dressing
Medium-Dry White Wine—Penedés
Lemon and Chicken
Hot Potatoes Canary Style
Bananas with Honey
Espresso Coffee with Licor 43

FROM GALICIA

Tuna and Scallions Canape (Tapas)
Dry White Wine—Castilla y León
Shrimp and Wine Omelet

Ham and Cabbage Soup
Hot Crunchy Bread
Almond Flan
Coffee and Lepanto Brandy

MIXED MENUS

Spain is a land of many cultural influences—from the earliest Celtic through the Phoenician, Roman, Arab, European, and New World influences. The foods of Spain reflect the contributions of all of these groups. Although this book is written to demonstrate regional cuisine, you can create wonderful meals by mixing recipes from different regions. There is no limit to what you and your imagination can do. I have put together several samples of mixed regional recipes that can take you on a culinary journey through several regions of Spain at one meal.

Dry Sherry (optional)—Jerez
Clams in Romesco Sauce (Tapas)
Summer Tuna Salad Andalucía Style
or Beans and Asparagus Soup with Ham
Dry White Wine—Rioja
Baked Red Snapper Fillets
Seafood-Flavored Rice
or Potatoes in Paprika Sauce
Rice Pudding
Coffee

Baked Clams with Rum (Tapas)
Lobster Soup with Tomatoes
A Robust, Dry, Full-Body Red Reserve—Rioja
Duck with Wine Sauce
Saffron Rice
or Cauliflower Muleteer Style
Classic Cheesecake
Coffee and Anís del Mono Sweet Anise Liqueur

Clams in Chili Sauce (Tapas)
Escarole with Olives and Cheese
Dry Red Wine—Rioja

Shellfish Medley in Saffron Sauce
Seafood-Flavored Rice
Heavenly Dessert
Espresso with Fundador Brandy

Carrots with Sherry Wine (Tapas)
Fish and Tomato Soup (optional)
Dry White Reserve—Castilla y León
Shrimp in Garlic Sauce (double the tapas recipe as a main dish)
White Rice and Sherry
or Saffron Rice
Almond and Walnut Custard
Espresso with Miguel Torres Orange Liqueur

BRUNCH MENUS

We Spanish love to eat a late breakfast or an early lunch. It's a leisurely meal that stretches the morning and eases into the afternoon. It goes with lots of coffee and friends and is always a most relaxing experience.

UNO
White Gazpacho with Grapes
Spanish Omelet
Peasant Bread
Strawberry Sherbet
Coffee

DOS
Medium-Dry Sherry
Apple and Pepper Salad
Vegetables with Ham and Eggs
Peasant Bread
Orange Cake Squares
Coffee

TRES
Dry Light White Wine—Rioja
Sole with Raisins (Tapas)
Three-Layer Omelet
Apple Preserves
Espresso Coffee

A TYPICAL SPANISH CHRISTMAS MENU

This menu is a Christmas feast. From tapas to dessert, each dish is a traditional favorite, and the recipes represent cooking from different regions of Spain. It's like all the members of a Spanish family coming together for a joyous holiday celebration. We Spanish love to party and eat, and at holiday time we get to do both. I hope you do, too.

Dry Sherry—Jerez
Mushrooms with Garlic and Sausage (Tapas)
Medium-Dry Sparkling Wine—Penedés
Christmas Red Cabbage
Garlic Egg Soup Castilian Style
Dry, Full-Body Red Reserve—Rioja
Turkey Andalucian Style
Seafood-Flavored Rice
Sautéed Artichokes
Heavenly Dessert
Espresso Coffee with Carlos I Brandy

TAPAS

Party time! Lots of nice people getting together for a good time. When it's at your house and you're looking for a great idea to make your party special, think tapas. These little appetizers are easy to prepare, colorful to serve, and they are *muy delicioso*. Tapas are the perfect beginning to a good time and are becoming one of the most popular dishes wherever people get together to enjoy themselves.

Baked Clams with Rum
Miniature Pizzas
Chorizos and Olives
Mussels in Parsley Sauce
Shrimp in Garlic Sauce
Hot Garlic Mayonnaise with Potatoes
Olives and Pine Nuts Canape
Shrimp Alioli Canape
Baked Clams and Chorizo
Grilled Beef with Garlic Mayonnaise
Hot Crunchy Bread for Sauce Dipping

SPANISH WINES, SHERRIES, AND LIQUEURS

Spain produces more wine than any other country. Every region of Spain, including the Canary and Balearic Islands, produces remarkable wines. Some are limited, such as the wines of Galicia, which are never exported since they are totally consumed by the Galicians. Asturias produces no grape wine but bottles *sidra*, a bubbly, delicious hard apple cider that is both refreshing and delightfully exhilarating. The great sherries of the world are produced in Andalucía and shipped to every country, as are the fresh, robust red and white wines of Levante and New Castile. Spain produces rare liqueurs like Licor 43 and Aguardiente, which are distilled from complicated ancient recipes, some of which are known only to a few men. The region of Catalonia produces a naturally fermented sparkling wine from the Penedés area called *cava*, the equal of most any champagne. It is the wines from the Rioja region of Old Castile, however, that have established Spanish wines among the best in the world. A perfect climate, pH-balanced soil, and a rich river create conditions perfectly suited to the cultivation of many grape varieties. Patient vintage techniques combined with strict industry standards have resulted in wines that are guaranteed to provide you with ultimate wine pleasure.

We Spanish say, "no meal is complete without a great Spanish wine," and there are many to choose from. Look for them in your local liquor store and add to the pleasure of your classic Spanish meal with a great wine from Spain. The following lists will help you choose.

SPARKLING WINES

CAVAS (Champagne Method)

LABEL	BODEGAS	AREA	CHARACTERISTICS
Lambey	Pedro Domecq	Penedés	Very Dry
Brut Clásico	Codorníu	Penedés	Very Dry
Carta Nevada	Freixenet	Penedés	Very Dry
Lambey Brut	Pedro Domecq	Penedés	Medium Dry

MOST POPULAR SPANISH WINES

LABEL	BODEGAS	AREA	CHARACTERISTICS
Gran Sangre de Toro 1979	Miguel Torres	Penedés	Dry, Full-Body Red Reserve
Marqués Arienzo Reserva 1983	Pedro Domecq	Rioja	Dry, Full-Body Red Reserve
Marqués Arienzo Gran Reserva 1981	Pedro Demecq	Rioja	Robust Dry, Full-Body Red Reserve
Gran Coronas Black 1977	Miguel Torres	Penedés	Dry, Full-Body Red
Lar de Barros Tinto Reserva 1988	Bodegas Inviosa	Extremadura	Dry, Full-Body Red Reserve
Viña Vial	Federico Paternina	Rioja	Dry, Full-Body Red
Martín Sancho Verdejo 1990–91	Bodegas Angel Rodriguez	Castilla y León	Dry, Full-Body Red
Marqués de Caseres	Marqués de Caseres	Rioja	Dry Light Red
Marqués de Arienzo Cosecha 1986	Pedro Domecq	Rioja	Dry Light Red
Privilegio	Pedro Domecq	Rioja	Dry Light Red
Tinto Pesquera 1989	Bodegas Alejandro Fernández	Castilla y León	Dry Light Red
Monte Sierra Tinto 1991	Bodegas Somontano	Aragón	Dry Light Red
Banda Azul	Federico Paternina	Rioja	Dry Light Red
Cabernet Sauvignon	Jean León	Penedés	Dry Light Red
Privilegio	Pedro Domecq	Rioja	Dry White

Banda Dorada	Federico Paternina	Rioja	Dry White
Marqués de Caseres	Marqués de Caseres	Rioja	Dry White
Marqués de Riscal	Marqués de Riscal	Castilla y León	Dry White
Chardonnay	Jean León	Penedés	Dry White
Reserva Limousine 1981	Marqués de Riscal	Castilla y León	Dry White Reserve
Marqués de Arienzo Blanco 1988	Pedro Domecq	Rioja	Dry Light White
Viña Esmeralda	Miguel Torres	Penedés	Medium Dry White
Marqués de Caseres	Marqués de Caseres	Rioja	Dry Rosé

POPULAR SHERRIES FROM THE REGION OF JEREZ

LABEL	BODEGAS	CHARACTERISTICS
La Ina	Pedro Domecq	Dry
Tio Pepe	González Byass	Dry
Fino Quintana	Osborne	Dry
Don Fino	Sandeman	Dry
Tico	Harvey	Dry
Double Century	Pedro Domecq	Medium Dry
Primero Amontillado	Pedro Domecq	Medium Dry
El Palacio	González Byass	Medium Dry
51 La Amontillado	Pedro Domecq	Medium Dry
Dos Cortados	Williams & Humbert	Medium Dry
Double Century	Pedro Domecq	Medium Sweet
Rio Viejo	Pedro Domecq	Medium Sweet
Royal Corregidor	Sandeman	Medium Sweet
Celebration Cream	Pedro Domecq	Sweet
Bristol Cream	Harvey	Sweet
Viña #25	Pedro Domecq	Sweet
El Palacio Cream	González Byass	Sweet

POPULAR SPANISH BRANDIES AND LIQUEURS

BRANDIES	BODEGAS	AREA	CHARACTERISTICS
Carlos I	Pedro Domecq	Jerez	Smooth
Fundador	Pedro Domecq	Jerez	Everyday Brandy
Lepanto	González Byass	Jerez	Smooth
Tres Torres	Miguel Torres	Penedés	Everyday Brandy

LIQUEURS

LIQUEURS	BODEGAS	AREA	CHARACTERISTICS
Licor 43	Diego Zamora	Cartagena	Sweet Citrus Taste
Miguel Torres Orange Liqueur	Miguel Torres	Penedés	Orange Brandy Liqueur
Anís del Mono	Vicente Bosch	Barcelona	Sweet Anise Taste

SANGRÍA

One of the most popular wine drinks throughout the world is sangría. It is a combination of red wine, fruit juices, ice, and soda. Sangría was introduced into Spain during the Roman occupation by a Roman soldier, Helio Gabala, said to be the first person to pour wine over ice. Recipes for sangría have become more than simply wine and ice. I offer this suggestion for Sangría a la Chef Ef as a thoroughly exciting combination of flavors and refreshment.

SANGRIA A LA CHEF EF

SERVES 6 – 8

2	cups (16 oz.) dry full-body red wine
2	tablespoons (1 oz.) brandy
½	cup orange juice
1	tablespoon sugar (optional)
1	cup seltzer or 7-Up

2   orange slices
2   lemon slices
2   lime slices
2   fresh mint leaves
2   cups ice

Combine all ingredients in a large pitcher and mix well. Refrigerate for about 20 minutes. Pour the sangría into wine glasses filled with ice and serve.

Note: For white sangría, follow the same steps above and replace the red wine with a dry white wine.

SPECIAL INGREDIENTS

ANISETTE   A sweet liqueur made of aniseed and flavored with aromatic herbs. Available at most liquor stores.

APPLE CIDER OR *SIDRA*   One of the oldest forms of beverage. It is produced by the fermentation of the juice of ripe cider apples. Available in most liquor stores.

BLANCH   To plunge vegetables or meat into boiling water for a given length of time, usually 3–5 minutes.

BUTIFARRAS   A pork sausage, highly seasoned with sweet herbs and spices. Italian sweet sausages can be used as a substitute.

CABRALES CHEESE   A blue cheese made of cow's milk, similar to Roquefort cheese but less strong. This cheese is aged in the mountain caves of Asturia in the northern part of Spain. Available through specialty food stores. Substitute: Roquefort or Bleu Cheese.

CARAMELIZE   To dissolve sugar adding water very slowly under low heat until a golden color.

CHORIZO   A Spanish sausage prepared with lean pork and flavored with garlic and sweet paprika. Available in some supermarkets or Latin stores. Imported from Spain is the best kind. Be sure that they are lean.

CILANTRO   An herb similar to flat parsley but having a very distinctive flavor. Also known as coriander and Chinese parsley. Available in most supermarkets.

CLAMS OR MUSSELS   One of the best methods to clean mussels or ·clams is by soaking them overnight in salted water and sprinkling them with bread crumbs. This procedure will ensure that they will release any salty material within the shells.

CRUSHED RED PEPPER This spice is dried, red, hot peppers crushed with their seeds which gives it an added spiciness.

FLAT PARSLEY This variety of parsley is the oldest of five known kinds. It has flat, bright green fan-shaped leaves with long stems. It has a milder taste than common curly parsley and retains its brightness when cooked. Use curly raw, flat cooked.

HOT PAPRIKA This spice is made from ground hot red peppers including the seeds.

LICOR 43 A brilliant, clear golden liqueur with the unforgettable flavor of citrus fruits. Available in most liquor stores.

MANCHEGO CHEESE Spain's best-known cheese from the land of Don Quixote. This cheese is made of 100 percent sheep's milk. Available in specialty food stores. Substitute: Provolone.

OLIVE OIL There are five different grades of olive oil: *Extra Virgin*, with an acidity level of 1 percent or less; *Fine Virgin*, with an acidity level of 1 percent to 1.5 percent; *Semi-Fine Virgin*, with an acidity level of 1.5 percent to 3 percent; *Pure* olive oil, which is obtained by mixing Virgin and Refined olive oils; finally, *refined* olive oil, which is created by a heat process resulting in less fragrance and lighter color. When cooking or sautéing use Pure or Refined olive oil. For dressings or cold sauces I recommend Fine or Semi-Fine Virgin olive oil. For salads use the Semi-Fine or Extra Virgin grade. Olive oil has no cholesterol and no more calories than vegetable oil. It is low in saturated fat and rich in monosaturated fat, vitamins A, D, E, and K. Olive oil can be kept for up to two years if properly capped and stored away from direct sunlight.

PAPRIKA A mildly flavored red powdered condiment prepared from sweet, deseeded red pepper. Available in most supermarkets.

PIMENTOS   Pimentos are really peppers . . . with a difference. The pepper involutes at the blossom end while the pimento grows to a point at the blossom end. Pimentos are always red, slightly sweeter, and seem to give up their skins easier in the roasting and peeling process.

PLANTAINS or *PLÁTANOS*   A vegetable that looks like a banana but cannot be eaten raw. It is harvested while green and is either fried or baked. It is used in both its unripe and ripe states. Available in most supermarkets.

QUESO DE RONCAL and IDIAZABAL   Two smoky, creamy low-fat cheeses produced from ewe's milk in the region of Navarra, Spain. A great substitute is domestic goat cheese.

ROSE WATER   An extract of rose petals used in sweet dishes. Available in most drugstores.

SAFFRON   A golden-colored spice from the stigma of the crocus flower. Great with Spanish rice dishes. It is also the most expensive spice in the world. Available in supermarkets. When buying saffron, look for the type that comes in threads.

SALTED DRIED COD FILLETS   An inexpensive dried fish very popular in the Basque Country. Available in most supermarkets.

SERRANO HAM   A cured ham similar to prosciutto ham. The only difference is that it is cured with olive oil and sweet paprika instead of black pepper, and it is less salty than its Italian counterpart. Available in some supermarkets and most Latin markets.

SHERRY   Spanish wines sometimes called *sherris, scheris, xerex, jerez,* or *sack*. Produced only in Spain, especially in the area of Jerez de la Frontera. Available in most liquor stores.

SOURCES FOR
SPANISH INGREDIENTS

Even though many supermarkets around the country have a section of Spanish foods, I have compiled a list of places by state where you can find some of the special ingredients in this book.

CALIFORNIA

Casa Lucas Market
2934 24th Street
San Francisco, CA 94110
(415) 826-4334

Casa Sanches
2778 24th Street
San Francisco, CA 94110
(415) 282-2400

El Mercado Grocery
3425 E. First Avenue
Los Angeles, CA 90063
(213) 269-2269

The Grand Central Market
317 South Broadway
Los Angeles, CA 90013
(213) 622-1763

La Raza Mercado
716 North Virgil Avenue
Los Angeles, CA 90029
(213) 663-5882

COLORADO

Johnnie's Market
2030 Larimer Street
Denver, CO 80205
(303) 297-0155

CONNECTICUT

La Placita del Pueblo
546 Park Street
Hartford, CT 06101
(203) 246-1825

FLORIDA

Ayestaran Supermarket
700 SW 27th Avenue
Miami, FL 33135
(305) 642-3539

La Aurora Super Market
341 SW 40th Avenue
Fort Lauderdale, FL 33317
(305) 583-9733

GEORGIA

Diaz Market
106 6th Street NE
Atlanta, GA 30308
(404) 872-0928

ILLINOIS

Casa Esteiro
2719 West Division
Chicago, IL 60622
(312) 252-5432

El Original Supermercado Cardenas
3922 North Sheridan Road
Chicago, IL 60607
(312) 525-5610

International Food Shop
1135 West Belmont Avenue
Chicago, IL 60657
(312) 525-7838

La Preferida Inc.*
3400 West 35th Street
Chicago, IL 60632
(312) 254-7200

La Casa del Pueblo
1810 South Blue Islands
Chicago, IL 60608
(312) 421-4640

Supermercado Gutierrez
1628 West Montrose Avenue
Chicago, IL 60613
(312) 271-7741

LOUISIANA

Latin Super Market
1800 North Broad Street
New Orleans, LA 70119
(504) 943-1988

MASSACHUSETTS

El Coloso Market
102 Columbia Street
Cambridge, MA 02139
(617) 491-1361

Tropical Foods, Inc.
2101 Washington Street
Boston, MA 02119
(417) 442-7439

MICHIGAN

Algo Especial
2628 Bagley Street
Detroit, MI 48216
(313) 963-9013

La Colmena
2443 Bagley Street
Detroit, MI 48216
(313) 237-0295

La Fiesta Market
3438 Bagley Street
Detroit, MI 48216
(313) 554-1168

Moreno's Market
425 Puritan Street
Detroit, MI 48203
(313) 554-1168

NEW JERSEY

Caridad del Cobre
115 Roseville Avenue
Newark, NJ 07107
(201) 482-1827

Corte & Co.*
414 Hoboken Avenue
Jersey City, NJ 07306
(201) 653-7246

NEW YORK

España Imports*
254-21 39th Avenue
Little Neck, NY 11363
(718) 932-9335

Grace's Marketplace*
1237 Third Avenue
New York, NY 10021
(212) 737-0600

H. Roth & Son*
1577 First Avenue
New York, NY 10028
(212) 734-1110

Ines Grocery*
269 Willis Avenue
Mineola, NY 11501
(516) 746-6637

International Groceries
5219 9th Avenue
New York, NY 10018
(212) 279-5514

Iron Gate Products*
424 West 54th Street
New York, NY 10019
(212) 757-2670

Latin American Products
142 West 46th Street
New York, NY 10036
(212) 302-4323

Sabro (La Mancha) International*
P.O. Box 1141
Woodstock, NY 12498
(914) 679-9651

OHIO

Spanish American Food Market
7001 Wade Park Avenue
Cleveland, OH 44103
(216) 432-2720

OREGON

Becerra Elda
108 NE 28th Avenue
Portland, OR 97232
(503) 233-6830

PENNSYLVANIA

El Botecito
401 West Cumberland Street
Philadelphia, PA 19133
(215) 634-8772

TEXAS

Fiesta Mart
5600 Mykawa Road
Houston, TX 77037
(713) 644-1611

Mendez Groceries
3725 McKinney Avenue
Dallas, TX 75204
(214) 521-5451

WASHINGTON, D.C.

American Grocery
1813 Columbia Road NW
Washington, D.C. 20009
(202) 265-7455

Casa Peña
1638 17th Street, NW
Washington, D.C. 20009
(202) 462-2222

WISCONSIN

El Paraiso Grocery
1407 S. 7th Street
Milwaukee, WI 53204
(414) 643-4949

El Rey
1023 S. 16th Street
Milwaukee, WI 53204
(414) 643-1640

*Sources of mail-order foods and catalogs.

Index

255